Cambridge Elements ≡

Elements in P₍
edited
James T.
The University of Br

G000079538

HUMAN COLOR VISION AND TETRACHROMACY

Kimberly A. Jameson
University of California, Irvine

Timothy A. Satalich
University of California, Irvine

Kirbi C. Joe
University of California, Irvine

Vladimir A. Bochko
University of Vaasa

Shari R. Atilano
University of California, Irvine

M. Cristina Kenney
University of California, Irvine

CAMBRIDGE
UNIVERSITY PRESS

CAMBRIDGE
UNIVERSITY PRESS

University Printing House, Cambridge CB2 8BS, United Kingdom

One Liberty Plaza, 20th Floor, New York, NY 10006, USA

477 Williamstown Road, Port Melbourne, VIC 3207, Australia

314–321, 3rd Floor, Plot 3, Splendor Forum, Jasola District Centre,
New Delhi – 110025, India

79 Anson Road, #06–04/06, Singapore 079906

Cambridge University Press is part of the University of Cambridge.

It furthers the University's mission by disseminating knowledge in the pursuit of
education, learning, and research at the highest international levels of excellence.

www.cambridge.org
Information on this title: www.cambridge.org/9781108714129
DOI: 10.1017/9781108663977

© Kimberly A. Jameson, Timothy A. Satalich, Kirbi C. Joe, Vladimir A. Bochko, Shari
R. Atilano, and M. Cristina Kenney 2020

This publication is in copyright. Subject to statutory exception
and to the provisions of relevant collective licensing agreements,
no reproduction of any part may take place without the written
permission of Cambridge University Press.

First published 2020

A catalogue record for this publication is available from the British Library.

ISBN 978-1-108-71412-9 Paperback
ISSN 2515-0502 (online)
ISSN 2515-0499 (print)

Cambridge University Press has no responsibility for the persistence or accuracy of
URLs for external or third-party internet websites referred to in this publication
and does not guarantee that any content on such websites is, or will remain,
accurate or appropriate.

Human Color Vision and Tetrachromacy

Elements in Perception

DOI: 10.1017/9781108663977
First published online: May 2020

Kimberly A. Jameson
University of California, Irvine

Timothy A. Satalich
University of California, Irvine

Kirbi C. Joe
University of California, Irvine

Vladimir A. Bochko
University of Vaasa

Shari R. Atilano
University of California, Irvine

M. Cristina Kenney
University of California, Irvine

Author for correspondence: Kimberly A. Jameson, kjameson@uci.edu

Abstract: Human color perception is widely understood to be based on a neural coding system involving signals from three distinct classes of retinal photoreceptors. This retinal processing model has long served as the mainstream scientific template for human color vision research and has also proven to be useful for the practical design of display technologies, user interfaces, and medical diagnostic tools that enlist human color perception behaviors. Recent findings in the area of retinal photopigment gene sequencing have provided important updates to our understanding of the molecular basis and genetic inheritance of individual variations of human color vision. This Element focuses on new knowledge about the linkages between color vision genetics and color perception variation and the color perception consequences of inheriting alternative, nonnormative, forms of genetic sequence variation.

Keywords: color perception, individual variation in normal color vision, perceptual color space dimensionality, photopigment opsin genotype

© Kimberly A. Jameson, Timothy A. Satalich, Kirbi C. Joe, Vladimir A. Bochko, Shari R. Atilano, and M. Cristina Kenney 2020

ISBNs: 9781108714129 (PB), 9781108663977 (OC)
ISSNs: 2515-0502 (online), ISSN 2515-0499 (print)

Contents

1 Introduction and Scope

The perception of color is an internal, highly subjective experience triggered by properties of light from the external world. An observer's color experience depends both on the properties of the nervous system devoted to color processing, which can vary considerably across individuals, and minor configural changes in viewing circumstances. Thus, despite the compelling salience of the perceived environmental colors we may experience while appreciating a magnificent natural scene, color experience should not be thought of as the act of simply registering features that exist in the world. Nor should it be thought of as an unbiased personal index of object properties. Rather, color is a product of observers' minds, existing as highly individualized constructions of each observer's visual apparatus and the specific ways it translates sensory information received from the world.

Despite this individual variation of color sensations, we can, however, predict the sensitivity ranges of "normal" human color experience if we examine how human color perception on average varies as a function of underlying biology and perceptual experience. Thus, rather than focus on the usual comparisons of how the sensations of a person with normal color vision differ from those of individuals with color vision anomalies or deficiencies, we might alternatively explore how color sensations vary between human observers who have normal, nondeficient, color vision capabilities compared to those who might be expected to experience nondeficient but "nonnormative" sensations of color vision. Toward this aim we discuss recently discovered genetic factors that can lead to potentially richer variations in color vision than have previously been assumed. By examining such factors we hope to enrich the narrative and general understanding of how individual differences in normal color sensations originate internally, and what such variation implies for color perception research, theory, and applications.

The research we review relates to a specific and rather exciting topic that has been referred to as "potential tetrachromacy" in current color vision research. Scientific advances since the 1990s have led to a better understanding of the relevance of both the genetic and physiological basis of color experience than ever before. Tetrachromacy, in its minimal sense, refers to the possession of four rather than three types of cone receptor cell classes in the photosensitive layer of the eyes. As detailed in the text that follows, recent research in molecular genetics, color perception, and cognitive psychology has clarified the underpinnings of human color sensations, how color experience has evolved, and the directions human color perception might follow in the future. Such research advances suggest that extensions of accepted color perception theory are called for to account for retinal photopigment diversity that is not integral to the accepted theory of color vision trichromacy.

1.1 Background

1.1.1 Why Do We Experience Color?

The ability to perceive color is so natural that we rarely consider its origin. Color perception, like perception of texture or motion, occurs when our visual system encounters information from illuminated objects. This ability to detect surface variation by sampling the light, or spectra, reflected off environmental objects is widespread across terrestrial species. Human color sensations are enjoyed by the processing of reflected spectra within a relatively narrow (~380 nm to ~740 nm) "visible" range of electromagnetic wavelengths. Color requires both (1) photon capture by photoreceptors and (2) encoding of photoreceptor excitation ratios.

The number of colors normal human individuals can distinguish varies but is generally estimated to be between 1 and 10 million. Perceived color variation is due to the ways our available photoreceptors react to reflected light. Knowledge of photoreceptor response sensitivities permits estimation of individual metameric color equivalence classes – or, object reflectance spectra that have different physical forms but produce the same color percept. The existence of natural and man-made metameric classes of reflectance spectra, and their variation vis-à-vis an observer's photopigments, are strong evidence that profiles of light reflected off objects are not uniquely colored. Indeed, object reflectance spectra are only electrical and magnetic pulses of photon energy waves, which do not contain any color or even have any visual features. Thus, the experience of color is an internal construction.

1.1.2 What Is Color Vision For?

Despite the nonunique mapping from color to reflected light, color cues are used in detecting targets against dappled backgrounds, perceptual segregation of objects from one another, and object identification and categorization. During nonhuman primate evolution, an ability to detect color differences between surfaces was likely selected for because it provided a means of signaling important information for the species. Perhaps color permitted the identification of carbohydrate-rich fruit or tender leaves (Mollon 1989; Osorio and Vorobyev 1996; Dominy and Lucas 2001; Regan et al. 2001; Lucas et al. 2003) or aided social interaction through detecting physiological states of conspecifics (Sumner and Mollon 2003; Changizi et al. 2006; Fernandez and Morris 2007).

The benefits of such color vision capabilities may have played an important role in the evolution of nonhuman primates into humans. Thus, although color is not a physical property of the world, and considerable color perception variation exists among humans, the ability to perceive color in the environment seems evolutionarily important. Because the perception of color is thought to be a flexible, evolved, capacity, investigation of its inherited biological basis and its trajectory in humans is of great interest.

1.1.3 The Genetic Basis of Color Vision

Human color vision is traditionally considered a capacity based on signals from three primary processing channels linked to neural signals produced by three different classes of photosensitive pigments found in human retinas (Liebmann 1972; Bowmaker and Dartnall 1980). These three types of neural signals from the eye are processed further by cortical mechanisms that typically maintain a modified coding of this three-channel arrangement (e.g., MacLeod 1985). Molecular genetics research has advanced the study of retinal processing by isolating the human genes responsible for the retina's photosensitive opsin pigments (Dartnall, Bowmaker, and Mollon 1983; Neitz and Jacobs 1986; Nathans, Thomas, and Hogness 1986b). Among these advances is the finding that genotypes can be quite diverse, such that it is common to observe more than three photopigment opsin variants and individuals expressing more than three retinal photopigment types (Neitz and Jacobs 1986, 1990; Merbs and Nathans 1992; Winderickx et al. 1992; Neitz, Neitz, and Jacobs 1993). Possessing more than three retinal photopigment classes is most common in females who are "heterozygous" for photopigment opsin genes (with different variants of a given gene on each X chromosome). The frequency of occurrence of opsin gene heterozygotes with four-photopigment retinal phenotypes in the Caucasian population has been estimated at between 47% and 50% (Neitz and Neitz 1998). Most surprisingly, it has been reported that men with normal color vision can have (Neitz, Neitz and Grishok 1995) and express genes for more than just two X-encoded cone pigments, with estimates of up to 8% of males expressing a four-photo-pigment retinal phenotype (Sjoberg et al. 1998).

Research documenting this rich diversity of color expression and experience has been hampered until recently by a lack of appropriate tools. Standard perceptual methods currently in use for identifying and screening color vision anomalies are not designed to detect perceptual variations that may arise in retinal tetrachromats. Thus, compared to well-known color vision differences arising from dichromacy, no standardized perceptual method exists for identifying retinal tetrachromats, and the precise nature of the perceptual differences possibly experienced by such observers is largely unknown.

Tool development in this area, furthermore, has been hampered by uncertainty concerning both (1) the prevalence of tetrachromats in the general population and (2) the extent to which retinal tetrachromacy might imply theoretical and practical perceptual impacts. As previously mentioned, our color experience begins with light from the visible portion of the electromagnetic spectrum stimulating human photoreceptors as object reflectance spectra and creating color sensations through comparisons of different photoreceptor class signals. The encoding of color via differences or "contrast" in receptor excitation is essential because a photoreceptor whose sensitivity distribution peaks around 530 nm communicates to the brain only the varying amounts of stimulating light it receives, not its wavelength composition. It only says, "I'm responding, I'm responding!" It does not communicate "I'm responding and I'm greenish!" The "greenish" part of the message comes when signals from different photoreceptor types are subsequently compared with one another in the neural circuitry beyond the retina.

The traditional theoretical treatment of color begins with the assumption that humans derive color information from responses of three cone classes containing different photopigments, distributed by the millions across the retina. These different cone classes are generated through expression of different opsin genes. Opsin genes with different amino acid sequences and a light-absorbing chromaphore can produce photoreceptor classes with drastically different absorption spectra, which perceptually relate to chromatic response functions described by color vision models.

This standard trichromatic view of color processing has been supported by much research. Genetic sequences identified for human light-sensitive pigments generally include three distinct groups of receptor types: (1) the chromosome-3-linked "rod" rhodopsin pigment (Sparkes et al. 1986) that responds maximally at low light levels and can interact with color vision; (2) the chromosome-7-linked short-wave sensitive "cone" photopigment; and (3) the X-chromosome-linked middle- and long-wave sensitive cone photopigments (Nathans et al. 1986b). Genes for the X-chromosome-linked photopigments are the basis for our color sensitivity at the mid- and long-wavelength portions of the visible spectrum. These are called M-opsins and L-opsins, respectively, and they share 98% gene sequence similarity (Gegenfurtner and Sharpe 1999; Jacobs 2008; Jacobs and Nathans 2009). These receptor classes are distributed throughout the retina in varying proportions, with the rods representing about 120 million receptors and the cone photoreceptor classes (S-, M-, and L-cones) representing roughly 6 million receptors – the minority (about 10%) of those being S-cones, and with the ratio of X-linked photopigments varying considerably across individuals.

The structure and function of X-linked opsin genes reveal much about their evolutionary purpose as a highly adaptive component of the visual system. Several genetic features support this idea. First, consider that the naturally occurring genetic variations, such as the ability to differentiate appearances of predominantly long-wavelength frequencies (e.g., loosely speaking, reddish colors) from medium-wavelength frequencies (e.g., greenish colors) arose in our primate ancestors via straightforward X-linked gene duplication – a key process in evolving new gene functions. Second, a single missing or different nucleotide in certain portions of the opsin gene sequence (called a single-nucleotide polymorphism, or SNP) is all that is required to produce dramatic shifts in the visual response to light by changing an amino acid of the expressed opsin protein. (Winderickx et al. 1992; Sanocki et al. 1993). Third, duplication, divergence, intra- and intergenic crossovers, and unequal recombination are all normal occurrences for M- and L-cone opsin genes. These opsin gene features contribute to differences in retinal photopigment response properties and would be expected to readily produce, for example, associated photoreceptor phenotype changes within the range defined by an M-cone class with peak responses around 530 nm (medium-wavelength sensitive, or MWS) and an L-cone class with peak responses around 560 nm (long-wavelength sensitive, or LWS). The potential for a virtual continuum of peak response sensitivities for X-linked photopigments would be expected to contribute to high variability of human color vision phenotypes and is presumably a feature that in the long run is subject to evolutionary selection pressure and adaptation.

Unexpectedly, as science in the area advanced starting in the 1980s and throughout the 1990s, the tidy fit of the standard normal trichromat model became uncertain – especially when identification of the recombinant DNA opsin gene sequences revealed unexpected M- and L-opsin gene variation (Nathans et al. 1986a, 1986b). Subsequent research into genotype–phenotype relations found many M- and L-opsin gene sequence variants were systematically linked to the variation in peak responses of photopigment absorption curves (Asenjo et al. 1994). Moreover, variations in color vision phenotypes were traceable to individual genetic sequence variations, so it became possible to use individual opsin genotype data to inform and investigate color vision behaviors associated with phenotype variation.

Initially one very interesting consequence of the X-linked inheritance pattern of these photopigments was the implication that individuals who possessed two X chromosomes (who in the main are female) may have two different variants of long-wavelength sensitive opsin genes (that is, a different form on each X chromosome), commonly referred to as an opsin gene "heterozygosity." Owing to gene expression mechanisms in play during embryonic development, individuals with two distinct forms of an L-photo-pigment thus have a genetic potential to express more than the usual three photopigment classes (Neitz and Neitz 1998, Sjoberg et al. 1998). In other words, an individual with normal S- and M-photopigment opsin genotypes, who additionally possesses two variant forms of L-photopigment opsin genes, would be expected to retinally express four distinct photopigment classes, which are considered as distinct SWS, MWS, L'WS, and LWS photoreceptor types.

A central question raised by such opsin gene findings concerns the color experience of individuals with more than three photopigment classes. For example, does heterozygosity of L- or M-opsin genes in individuals with normal color vision result in (1) a modified form of trichromat color perception that confers enhanced normal color vision? Or is the consequence instead (2) some form of functional tetrachromacy? Either of these possibilities could translate into better-than-normal chromatic discrimination for the heterozygote individual, when compared to male or female normal trichromats. In our own research on this topic (e.g., Jameson et al. 2001) we have considered the possibility that females heterozygous for opsin genes are such individuals. Our hypothesis is that these individuals – called retinal tetrachromats – may express four retinal cone classes (in addition to rods that respond primarily at low levels of illumination), with each cone class offering different spectral response peaks and sensitivity distributions, such that these individuals have, at a minimum, the retinal potential to experience tetrachromatic vision (Mollon 1992).

1.2 Standard Color Vision Theory and Color Perception

Historically, human color vision has been modeled in individuals as a system based on signals from three different classes of retinal photorecep-tors, each of which responds selectively to energy from the short-, med-ium-, and long-wavelength regions of the visible electromagnetic spectrum.

Such signal processing is the basis for coding normal color vision "tri-chromacy," and as a color perception model trichromacy has served for decades as the theoretical foundation for advancing color perception research and the framework for essentially all the myriad of technologies developed for contemporary color display user-interface applications. While normal human color vision trichromacy is most typical, a color-deficient phenotype, known as color vision dichromacy (or "Daltonism") has been widely understood as an inherited trait since about the 1800s (Dalton 1798).

1.2.1 Color-Deficient Dichromats Reveal Color Vision Inheritance Mechanisms

While a small number of dichromats arise due to pathology or injury, most so-called "color-blind" dichromat individuals typically inherit their color vision deficit as a result of abnormal opsin gene features that result in the expression of only two classes of retinal photoreceptors, unlike the usual three classes, found in normal color vision processing.

As suggested in Section 1, since the 1990s information about the genetic basis for dichromacy and other forms of anomalous and normal color vision variation has advanced substantially, and the genetic sequence changes under-lying varying photoreceptor response properties have been greatly clarified. In contrast to the extensive, established literature on color vision deficiency, there is a comparatively smaller, although now growing, body of research on color vision performance expertise. This Element focuses on the perceptual conse-quences of nondeficient forms of color processing variation. The actual extent of normal color vision diversity has only been uncovered somewhat recently by investigations that both (1) examine the genetic sequences underlying the retinal photopigments, and (2) connect sequence variations to color perception behaviors arising from the expressed retinal phenotype. Here we survey empiri-cal results that show how color perception can vary across normal color vision observers when individuals with trichromat photopigment opsin genotypes are compared to female potential tetrachromat individuals. These are observers with a genetic potential for expressing the four distinct photopigment classes underlying retinal "tetrachromacy" (Nagy et al. 1981; Jordan and Mollon 1993; Jameson et al. 2001; Bosten et al. 2005; Jordan et al. 2010).

Jameson and colleagues have empirically shown that potential tetrachromats – who are those observers who possess photopigment opsin genotypes that permit expression of more than three retinal photopigment classes – systematically exhibit predictable color perception variations that differ from the variations seen among normal color vision control observers that possess genotypes typically associated with trichromat color vision phenotypes (Jameson 2009, Jameson et al. 1998a, 1998b, 2001, 2006, 2015, 2016; Bimler et al. 2004; Sayim et al. 2005; Bochko and Jameson 2018). Additional tetrachromacy research of note is reviewed below.

For the remainder of Section 1 we summarize the opsin genetics detail underlying potential human tetrachromat phenotypes. In Section 2 we review some recent empirical evidence relating to human tetrachromacy and how it may differ from normal trichromatic color perception, while emphasizing key findings that have pointed to both the potential for human tetrachromat differences and the empirically observed perceptual implications. We next summarize, in Section 3, our new empirical approach that provides full opsin genotyping profiles for each participant (Atilano et al. 2017, 2020). Then we describe our empirical assessment methods, data analyses, and the modeling approaches used with a new color reproduction task designed to investigate perceptual correlates of potential tetrachromat genotypes. In the empirical portion we present summary analyses of recently collected data to determine whether results from previously described machine learning approaches (Bochko et al. 2017; Bochko and Jameson 2018; Jameson et al. 2018) and a color reproduction performance model, which employs perceptual color space metrics (Satalich 2015), can be used to identify and model individuals with genetically tuned forms of color perception associated with tetrachromat phenotypes. Also in Section 3, the results are compared to data from trichromat genotype control individuals and are discussed with respect to patterns of color perception variation and opsin gene sequence markers that allow the expression of more than one type of L-cone photopigment variant (Bochko and Jameson 2018; Jameson et al. 2018). In Sections 4 and 5 implications of our findings are discussed in the context of the existing potential tetrachromacy research and we explore possible avenues for future research into human tetrachromacy.

1.3 Details of Color Vision Genetics

Photopigment opsin gene sequences provide the instructions for making a protein that is essential for normal color vision (Gegenfurtner and Sharpe 1999; Nathans et al. 1986a, 1986b; Jacobs 2008; Jacobs and Nathans 2009). This protein is found in the retina, which is the light-sensitive tissue at the back of the eye. The retina contains two types of light receptor groups, called rods and cones, which transmit visual signals from the eye to the brain. Rod cells are maximally sensitive in low-light conditions, or scotopic light levels. Cones respond primarily in bright light, or photopic levels, and are responsible for color vision. There are three types of cone classes, each containing a specific pigment (a photopigment called an opsin) with distinct response profiles that maximally respond to different wavelengths of light.

Research on the genetic basis of retinal photopigments has enabled an understanding of the biochemical explanation for photopigment response sensitivity as well as the genetic basis for individual differences in color perception. In general, results suggest that the majority of color vision in humans and Old World primates is trichromatic, being based on three classes of photopigments that are maximally sensitive to "red" (560–565 nm), "green" (530–535 nm), and "blue" (420– 430 nm) light (Bowmaker et al. 1978, 1991; Dartnall et al. 1983; Schnapf et al. 1987, 1988). The three photopigment opsins, as well as rhodopsin (the light-sensitive pigment active at low-light conditions found in the retina rod receptors), are heptahelical proteins, composed of seven transmembrane α-helices that are linked by intra- and extracellular loops. Visual excitation following photon absorption occurs as the result of 11-*cis* to all-*trans* isomerization of the chromophore located at a binding site in helix 7.

The genes encoding the opsins or apoproteins of the human red and green photopigments are each composed of six exons and are arranged in a head-to-tail tandem array located on the q-arm of the X chromosome (Nathans et al. 1986a, 1986b; Vollrath et al. 1988; Feil et al. 1990). Individuals with normal color vision usually have one red opsin gene in the proximal position of the gene array and one or more green opsin genes. These X-linked opsin genes have 98% identity in nucleotide sequence (including introns and 3' flanking regions) (Zhao et al. 1998). The mainstream view is that encoded MWS and LWS opsin apoproteins differ by an estimated 15 residues, 7 of which occur at positions (116 on exon 2, 180 on exon 3; 230, 233 on exon 4; 277, 285, 309 on exon 5) that ultimately influence photoreceptor responsivity in the expressed phenotype (Nathans et al. 1986a; Jacobs, 1998; Neitz and Neitz 2011; reviewed in Nathans et al. 1992; Asenjo et al. 1994). Other photopigment gene-specific amino acids recently investigated as impacting color perception involve positions 65, 111, 116 on exon 2; 153, 171, 174, 178, 180 on exon 3; and 230, 233, 236 on exon 4 (Dees et al. 2015).

The LWS gene sequence provides instructions for making an opsin pigment that is, generally speaking, more sensitive to regions of the visible spectrum associated with yellow/orange/red perceptions (i.e., long-wavelength light). In response to light stimulation, the photopigment triggers a series of chemical reactions within an L-cone. These reactions ultimately alter the cell's electrical charge, generating a signal that is transmitted to the brain. The brain combines input from all three types of cones to produce normal color vision. The LWS gene is located next to another opsin pigment gene, MWS, on the X chromosome. Roughly speaking, the MWS gene provides instructions for making a photopigment maximally sensitive to light at middle wavelengths (light perceived as yellow/green).

Most people have one copy of the LWS gene and one or more copies of the MWS gene on each X chromosome. A nearby region of DNA, known as the locus control region (LCR), regulates the activity of opsin gene expression. Theory suggests that the two opsin pigment genes nearest the LCR – which generally are the LWS gene and the first copy of the MWS gene – are the ones that are expressed in the phenotype and are thereby active in the retina and contribute to color vision.

1.3.1 Gene Sequence Variation Produces Changes in Color Perception

Human genotype/perceptual-phenotype analyses show that genotypic variation corresponds to shifts in the absorption spectra of expressed retinal pigments (Merbs and Nathans 1992a, 1992b, 1993; Asenjo et al. 1994), with concomitant shifts in observers' peak perceptual spectral sensitivity, or "λ-max," (Neitz, Neitz, and Jacobs 1991, 1995; Winderickx et al. 1992).

More specifically, it has been shown that specific single amino acid substitutions at codons 180 in exon 3, and codons 277 and 285 in exon 5, produce large shifts in phenotypic spectral sensitivity whereas the amino acids at codons 230 and 233 in exon 4 produce smaller shifts (Merbs and Nathans 1992a; Asenjo et al. 1994). The specific amino acids occurring at codons 180, 277, and 285 are highly conserved in vertebrates, showing that the sequences have been maintained throughout speciation that occurred during vertebrate evolution. The specific residues occurring at each position are associated with predictable shifts in λ-max for each species. Substitutions of amino acid residues involve the gain or loss of a hydroxyl-bearing group. Substitutions of hydroxyl groups at key positions are associated with shifts in photopigment response sensitivity toward shorter wavelengths of the visible spectrum. Mammals whose MWS and LWS genes demonstrate codon conservation at these key residues include cat, deer, guinea pig, horse, squirrel, goat, rabbit, dolphin, mouse, rat, and several species of New World monkeys (Zhou et al. 1997; Shyue et al. 1998; Yokoyama and Radlwimmer 1999).

In contrast to the highly conserved relationship between the amino acids at codons 230, 233, 277, and 285 and human perception of light as reddish or greenish, the specific amino acid occurring at codon 180 in the L-cone photopigment opsin gene is variable or polymorphic in *Homo sapiens* (Asenjo et al. 1994; Sharpe et al. 1998). Thus, generally in males of European ancestry, investigations show comparably similar observed frequencies of amino acids serine and alanine in position 180 of the LWS, or "red," opsin gene (Winderickx et al. 1992; Sharpe et al. 1998). By comparison, allelic variation is somewhat less common in position 180 of the MWS, or "green" gene, with the frequency of serine observed at 8% (with alanine occurring at 84%) of individuals (Sanocki et al. 1993).

Substitution of a hydrophobic residue for a hydroxyl-bearing amino acid at codon 180 produces a relatively large shift in λ-max in the LWS photopigment, but a lesser shift in λ-max in the MWS photopigment. Individuals with the more common serine at codon 180 in their LWS opsin gene will demonstrate an average spectral response, or λ-max, of approximately 557 nm for red light. Individuals inheriting alanine at codon 180 in their LWS gene demonstrate a 4–5 nm shift in their average λ-max for red light to 552 nm, moving their spectral sensitivity for red light toward the λ-max for green light, which is about 532 nm (Jacobs 1998; Sharpe et al. 1998).

Human females who have an extra retinal photopigment are most likely to have, in addition to normal SWS and MWS photopigments, two LWS pigments – one with L-180-serine and a second with L-180-alanine. Figure 1a depicts a schematic representation of a trichromat model with typical S-, M-, and L-cone responses, compared to that of a modeled observer possessing the genes for obligate expression of four distinct photoreceptor classes (Figure 1b), which provides a potential for color vision tetrachromacy, also referred to as a "potential tetrachromat."

Complicating further the analysis of the relationship between genotype and perceptual behavior is the chromosomal location of the MWS and LWS genes. The MWS and LWS photopigment opsin genes occur in a tandem array on the X chromosome. Females have two X chromosomes while males have a single X chromosome. Hence, females have two sets of such genes, one on each X chromosome, whereas males, with only one X chromosome, have only one set of genes. As a result, females have potentially greater genetic variability in their MWS and LWS photopigment gene combination than is possible for males. Whereas there are four possible MWS/LWS genotype combinations at codon 180 for males, there are nine possible MWS/LWS genotype combinations for females. Thus, based on the reasoning that greater genotype diversity increases the diversity of expressed phenotypes, it might be reasonable to expect color perception variation in females that is not found in phenotypes that arise from male photopigment opsin genotypes.

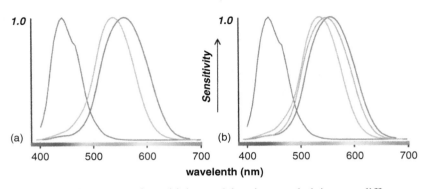

Figure 1 Cone spectral sensitivity model variants underlying two different observer types. The horizontal axis shows a color gradient approximating percepts of stimulus dominant wavelengths. The vertical axis shows cone responses normalized to a maximum of unity on a radiance scale. Functions show estimated spectral sensitivities of the L-cone class (red line), the M-cones (green line), and the S-cones (blue line) each normalized to peak at unity. (a) Shows trichromat cone basis functions implied by a normal color vision model from a three-photopigment genotype. Trichromat cone responses are based on the Smith and Pokorny (1975) cone fundamentals (see Stockman and Sharpe 2000 and http://www.cvrl.org/data base/text/cones/sp.htm). (b) Shows a potential tetrachromat with a schematic generalization of commonly found extra L-cone codon-180 opsin variation (the orange line) that is known to impact color perception. Opsin genotyping can be used to model and predict individual variations similar to (a) and (b) that are expressed as retinal phenotypes.

2 Investigating Color Perception in Individuals with Normal Photopigment Variations

Even before the X-chromosome opsin gene sequences for human color vision photopigments were isolated (Nathans et al. 1986a, 1986b) researchers strove to investigate normal color processing using trichromat observers with familial inheritance patterns associated with photopigment opsin genotypes, whom thereby had an obligate genetic potential for phenotypically expressing four distinct retinal photoreceptor types (Nagy et al. 1981).

One of the first empirical investigations into human tetrachromacy was actually conducted before human opsin genotyping was available, by Nagy et al. (1981), who reported results for a number of female candidates for tetrachromat genotypes compared to female and male trichromat controls. Because the Nagy et al (1981) investigations predated the isolation of photopigment opsin gene sequences, they used inheritance patterns for color vision anomalies as a marker for identifying women who were obligate carriers of genes for anomalous color vision, as evidenced by their color anomalous sons or fathers.

Standard instruments that use *anomaloscope matching* tasks are widely employed for identifying color vision deficiencies and characterizing the amount of deviation an observer exhibits compared to a normal color vision model (Birch 2001). Anomaloscopes are optical instruments in which an observer evaluates (by monocular viewing through an eyepiece) a circular split-field stimulus and manipulates stimulus control knobs to match the colors seen in two semicircular hemifields in both color and brightness. Anomaloscopes are used in research, applied industrial, and medical settings for the diagnosis of color vision defects. Diagnosis of X-chromosome-linked deficiencies specifically make use of the Rayleigh Match anomaloscope task, which requires observers to match a monochromatic yellow appearance, that is held constant in one hemifield, by balancing a blend of red and green primaries and brightness in the adjacent hemifield (Birch 2001).

Nagy et al. (1981) employed a novel variation on the usual anomaloscope Rayleigh-type matching procedure that involved a bipartite field in which a subject adjusted a central yellow mixture of uniform red (660 nm) and green (546 nm) lights to match a monochromatic yellow light (588 nm) in the adjacent split-half field.

The empirical goal was to evaluate whether individual's match settings remained the same under different adaptation states – a criterion for demonstrating trichromat additivity in this task – they tested these mixtures in three ways to view consistency of matching across adaptation states. The prediction was that trichromats should replicate match settings across all three conditions, whereas non-trichromats would not replicate match settings across conditions. They obtained mixtures in a context-free condition without a surrounding adapting annulus, as well as in two other conditions that respectively embedded Rayleigh mixtures in the different contexts of two large chromatic annuli (a blue, 455 nm, and a red, 670 nm, adapting light).

Comparing individual settings of study participants across all three matching conditions, Nagy and colleagues found that 19 males and 17 females (of 21 sampled) were "additive" across all three tested conditions. Observing additivity of trichromatic matches for an individual observer implies that only three different visual pigments are operative and needed to accurately match across the tasks. However, from among the 21 females sampled, 4 females, who reported incidence of familial color deficiency and were carrying a simple anomaly (the most common), set ranges of acceptable mixture ratios under neutral adaptation that did not overlap with the acceptable mixture ratios on one or both of the biased adaptation states. For these heterozygotes this indicates that two fields that matched under unbiased adaptation do not continue to match under biased adaptation, and this is a clear violation of the additivity law, which strongly implies color space dimensional differences across the observer groups studied.

In short, the data of Nagy et al. revealed color perception variations suggesting that at least some genetically-based color processing phenotypes – namely, mothers of color vision anomalous males – were likely to exhibit certain failures of Rayleigh match trichromat additivity. This hinted strongly of the possibility that these individuals possessed an extra photoreceptor class variant in their retinas. Indeed, Nagy and colleagues interpreted this finding as suggesting that the eyes of their heterozygous female participants contained more than the usual three normal cone pigments with different spectral sensitivities.

Although the investigation of Nagy et al. (1981) was restricted to the narrow region of color appearance space accessible with a modified Rayleigh-match task, the results of Nagy et al. can be viewed as the initial demonstration of "weak tetrachromacy" in humans, which we now know is not actual dimensional tetrachromacy (cf. Jacobs 2018, p. 111). In addition, Nagy et al. proposed the innovative notion of functional tetrachromacy (or "strong tetrachromacy" as described by Jordan and Mollon 1993) as something worthy of consideration in the modeling of human color appearance space.

One conservative interpretation of the results of Nagy et al. is that retinal or "weak" tetrachromacy, at a minimum, interferes with the ability of potential tetrachromats to repeat match mixture settings when producing mixtures with fewer than four variables. Thus, although skeptics of retinal tetrachromat potential may disagree with such an interpretation, the data of Nagy et al. show that some potential tetrachromats clearly differed from standard normal trichromats when tested using the classical psychophysical procedure they employed.

As elaborated in the text that follows, it should also be noted that other factors are likely to influence the empirical demonstration of human tetrachromat processing variations. These include complexities of color experience associated with increases in stimulus size, and scene and viewing complexity. For example, small-field monocularly viewed stimuli, of the kind used in standardized anomaloscope assessment procedures, by definition impose empirical constraints on detecting likely perceptual impacts that could arise from judgments made under binocular viewing of higher-dimensional stimulus variation. The more naturalistic conditions of binocular viewing and contextualized scenes allow for greater processing complexity and are thus more likely to uncover tetrachromacy. Indeed, increased stimulus complexity is what Nagy et al. sought to approximate when they used the nonstandard configuration of a large parafoveal match stimulus that was embedded in annular chromatic contexts. Thus, it is reasonable to expect that the empirical detection of human tetrachromacy is (1) more likely to occur under complex stimulus and viewing conditions; and (2) that the extent of its perceptual impact varies across color appearance space, and these expectations raise the question of how to best design an empirical investigation to uncover a tetrachromat processing variation should it exist.

2.1 Empirical Approaches for Identifying Tetrachromatic Color Perception

One advantage of the studies summarized earlier is that they employ well-established and standardized empirical psychophysical procedures to investigate color vision variations associated with extra photopigments. This allows potential tetrachromacy to be compared directly with data from mainstream color vision research. However, my collaborators and I have argued that to fully characterize the impact of a fourth photoreceptor class, novel empirical designs are required. These should ideally involve multiprimary devices (involving four primaries or greater) that employ viewing circumstances that are contextually richer than those provided by standard Maxwellian view or anomaloscope stimulus formats (Jameson et al. 2001; Jameson 2009). We have also suggested that, at a minimum, such empirical designs should explicitly enlist influences of chromatic and luminance contrast variation and changes in adaptation state, and assess binocular color appearance judgments, to maximize the chance of detecting and empirically quantifying the kind of color appearance differences that might be conferred by a fourth functional retinal photopigment class (Jameson et al. 2001, 2015, 2016; Sayim et al. 2005).

Following the early investigation of Nagy et al. (1981), a considerable amount of systematic research clarified possible retinal phenotype and color vision processing consequences arising from identified potential tetrachromat genotypes. To address the issue, a number of investigations starting in the mid- to late 1990s used various standardized psychophysical paradigms based on established color vision assessment techniques, such as color sorting tasks using stimuli from standardized color vision assessment tests, anomaloscope matching tasks, wavelength discrimination, and color matching (Sanocki et al. 1993; He and Shevell 1995; Shevell et al. 1997, 1998; Bimler et al. 2004; Hood et al. 2006; Jameson et al. 2006; Sun and Shevell 2008; Bimler and Kirkland 2009; Jordan et al. 2010; Konstantakopoulou et al. 2012; Dees and Baraas 2014).

Awareness of empirical considerations that might impact the chance of detecting color processing differences associated with tetrachromat retinas (some mentioned earlier) led a number of tetrachromacy investigators to explore using increased stimulus complexity, which allow for examination of more natural processing conditions and behaviors (Jameson et al. 1998a, 1998b, 2001, 2006, 2015, 2016; Bimler et al. 2004; Sayim et al. 2005; Bochko and Jameson 2018). These investigations used molecular genetic methods to identify potential retinal tetrachromats and found differences in perceptual behaviors when a genetic potential existed for more than three photopigment classes. Behaviors that differentiated potential tetrachromats from trichromat controls included perceiving more colors in diffracted spectra (Jameson et al. 2001); performance variation on a standardized test for trichromacy that was correlated with indices of richer color experience (Jameson et al. 2006); and color similarity and color naming patterns showing cognitive color processing variation among potential tetrachromats (Sayim et al. 2005). Although such investigations were not designed to address underlying color vision neural mechanisms or specify forms of "weak" or "strong" tetrachromacy, their results do show that using empirical conditions that approximate more naturalistic viewing circumstances (e.g., binocular viewing and contextualized stimuli) makes tetrachromacy more apparent, and that the genetic potential to express more than three cone classes is statistically correlated with differences in color categorization, naming, and color similarity judgments.

The push to make stimulus features more "realistic" is compatible with the view that there is merit in securing generalizability of color perception in the laboratory to that in real-world circumstances. For example, in the 1990s there was growing appreciation that color appearance studies should aim to use stimulus complexity that went beyond an annular color stimulus in an otherwise dark surround. It was argued that formats should attempt to approximate the configural features and relational structures that are commonly present in the realistic viewing of environmental scenes (Mausfeld and Niederée 1993).

This argument for enriching psychophysical stimuli beyond the usual monocularly viewed Maxwellian annulus formats was shown both formally and empirically to be highly relevant for modeling color perception (Mausfeld and Niederée 1993, and later Gordon and Abramov 2008). Since then, arguments in favor of *ecologically valid* psychophysical tests have gained support and it is now the approach that has become integral to our empirical tetrachromacy research (Jameson et al. 2001, 2016; Sayim et al. 2005; Jameson 2009; Bochko et al. 2017; Bochko and Jameson 2018).

A noteworthy investigation by Jordan and Mollon (1993) can be viewed as the beginning of what might be called *tetrachromacy-friendly* empirical tools and designs. Jordan and Mollon reported that among 31 obligate carriers, one woman (participant cDA7) was shown to be " ... in play as a candidate tetrachromat in the strong sense" (Jordon and Mollon 1993, p. 1505). Their results suggested that evidence for functional or "strong tetrachromacy" could be found using a ratio-matching (i.e., context-dependent) Rayleigh-type anomaloscope task. This study can therefore be considered the first to find evidence for "strong tetrachromacy" in human color vision for one specific color space region (yellow), implying that the detection of functional human tetrachromacy was empirically realizable and worthy of further investigation.

A second significant empirical advance for potential tetrachromacy was reported more recently by Jordan et al. (2010). These authors system-atically investigated both Rayleigh-type stimulus matching (3-AFC perfor-mance version of the Rayleigh match test for yellowish color appearances) and novel surface color triadic comparison judgments of greenish color appearances. Surface color triad tasks are widely recognized as useful for differentiating observers who vary by color vision phenotype (Shepard and Cooper 1992) and linguistic group (Moore et al. 2002). The triadic surface color judgments of Jordan et al. (2010) used 15 stimuli specifically designed to be dimensionally salient and differentiable by carriers of deuteranomaly and deuteranomalous observers, while simultaneously being nondifferentiable to normal color vision observers. Jordan et al. (2010) thus obtained data from observers' surface color triadic comparison choices that were analyzed using multidimensional scaling to quantify and model individual's judged dissimilarity among the 15 greenish stimuli they employed, and to determine their relative placement in each participant's personal color appearance space.

Extending tetrachromacy results from earlier triad experiments (Bimler et al. 2004; Sayim et al. 2005; Bimler and Kirkland 2009), the results of Jordan et al. (2010) convincingly showed that one female carrier of deuteranomaly (cDa29) clearly exhibited tetrachromatic color perception behavior that differentiated her from normal trichromat controls on a number of tasks and color processing measures (Jordan et al. 2010). Thus, similar to Jordon and Mollon's (1993) earlier findings for participant cDA7 in relation to Rayleigh-match yellow appearances, the findings for participant cDa29 suggest that for both Rayleigh-match yellow and for a small set of greenish surface color appearances, observer cDa29 exhibits a functional form of tetrachromacy. Such variation was predicted using a phenotype model based on specific photopigment opsin genotype information obtained through analyses of cDa29's X-chromosome opsin gene sequences (Jordan et al. 2010).

Beyond demonstrating functional tetrachromacy in specific yellowish and greenish regions of color appearance space, the results of Jordan et al. (2010) are significant in that they support earlier suggestions that emphasized the importance of using naturalistic, contextually rich, binocularly viewed surface color appearances to empirically assess potential human tetrachromacy (Jameson et al. 2001, 2006, 2016; Bimler et al. 2004; Sayim et al. 2005). Jordan et al. (2010) also defined and verified a research procedure for investigating perceptual color space variation that can be used in future research to clarify color perceptual processing impacts arising in other forms of opsin genotype variants. This advance is obviously valuable for systematically characterizing larger numbers of potential tetrachromats for genotype-based color appearance variation across large ranges of luminance and chromatic contrast for the entire perceptual color space (i.e., beyond yellow and green appearances).

Recent evidence therefore supports the idea that nondeficient individual variation in color perception is correlated with X-linked opsin genotypes that permit the expression of more than three distinct classes of photosensitive receptors in the human retina. Supporting data have accrued since the original results of Nagy et al. in 1981, and information linking genotypes to retinal phenotypes has advanced significantly. Knowledge has also advanced substantially on a number of genetic issues relating to phenotype expression of multiple photopigment variants; the consequences of possessing more than one, or multiple copies of, mutated allelic variations; and the consequences of hybrid genotypes and the highly biased retinal expression of a given cone class.

Recent advances in domain of adaptive optics also now permit the visualization of functioning photopigment classes in the mosaics of the living human retina (Carroll et al. 2005; Pircher and Zawadzki 2017). Even so, differentiation of the numerous X-linked photopigment variants remains difficult because measuring spectral response properties of different photopigments *in vivo* is very challenging and is complicated by a number of individually varying factors such as photopigment spectral-peak response proximity, optical density of pigments, cell "wave-guiding" morphology, and ocular media filtering. Nevertheless, because variations in color vision phenotypes are ultimately traceable to genetic variation, the use of individual opsin-genotype data to investigate behaviors associated is an important first step in characterizing color vision phenotype variation.

It is important to acknowledge that the retinal genotype–phenotype relationship is not deterministic (Crognale et al. 1998). Nonetheless, individual opsin-genotype data are now recognized as a defining basis for potential human tetrachromacy and so these data open up new research possibilities. For example, by carefully studying potential tetrachromats as minority individuals within the full spectrum of human color vision, we are likely to advance current scientific understanding of all forms of human color perception.

Moreover, data from these individuals should improve upon the standard observer models of trichromat color vision by further clarifying the relationships between potential tetrachromat genotypes and other early visual processing factors (i.e., macular pigmentation, trans-retinal photopigment optical density, preretinal filtering). In general, such standard observer model improvements are important since the observed relative perceptual processing impacts from tetrachromacy will help clarify the basis for known individual color perception variations found across normal trichromat color vision phenotypes. Finally, detailing the effects of retinal tetrachromacy on perception is needed to model the cognitive and perceptual processing features that ultimately could serve to identify behavioral markers for easily assessing color vision tetrachromacy. In the text that follows we detail novel empirical investigations that explore these issues.

3 An Empirical Investigation of Tetrachromacy

3.1 Rationale

In this Section we present an empirical investigation that addresses a long-standing and fundamental issue in color vision: Namely, are heterozygous females with tetrachromatic retinas functionally trichromatic (i.e., tetrachromat retinas do not alter "standard normal" color experience), or, alternatively, are they functionally tetrachromatic (i.e., tetrachromacy alters perceptual experience in ways that are not accounted for by the usual normal color vision models)? If we find support for the first option it would imply that trichromatic experience is strictly determined by processing that occurs at post-receptoral sites (e.g., the cortex). Alternatively, if we find support for functional tetrachromacy it implies that the post-receptoral color system is sufficiently variable and plastic enough to be able to take advantage of additional information provided by an extra photoreceptor class.

Answering this question is important because a convincing answer either way would contribute further to our understanding of how primate color vision evolved and of the dynamic potential underlying human color vision.

Tetrachromacy research is also likely to advance our understanding of the biological basis of color vision and color vision mechanisms that contribute to individual differences in color perception, thereby clarifying answers to the question of gender differences in color perception and behavior which have been hinted at in the cognitive psychology literature for a very long time.

The present investigations extend our previous research and build on the tetrachromacy research we have reviewed in two ways. First, the studies seek to employ rigorous methods that others may be able to use in future investigations. Second, the studies aim to minimize those empirical constraints that might limit the demonstration of functional tetrachromat processing differences. To do this we assess naturalistic, binocularly viewed, contextually embedded, surface colors with color similarity judgments obtained using a modified color-matching task.

Our approach is to obtain data that permits assessment of color appearance similarity relations through mapping and quantification of target-stimulus-to-matched-sample dissimilarities in each participant's personal color appearance space (Jameson et al. 1998a, 1998b, 2001, 2006; Bimler et al. 2004; Sayim et al. 2005). We will also take advantage of important contributing factors to color perception by studying individual differences among our study participants with regard to their ability to accurately reproduce colors. Individual differences in the ability to artistically reproduce colors displayed in naturalistic scenes allows us to explore associations between experiential and genetic factors thought to underlie individual color perception variation, such as perceptual learning and expertise, and photopigment opsin genetics (Jameson et al. 2015, 2016; Bochko and Jameson 2018).

Because empirical investigations that employ surface color perception have been shown to be particularly useful for investigations of potential tetrachromacy, the present research sought to extend this approach to explore how genetically based individual variation in color vision might relate to color perception phenotype – including practical and artistic uses of color appearance. The aim is to identify novel, ecologically valid, empirical measures of individuals' perceptual color experience that serve to clarify individual variations in underlying features and mechanisms of visual processing.

3.1.1 Rationale for the Retinal Opsin Genotyping

To characterize the photopigment opsin genotypes of our experimental subjects we conducted opsin genotyping analyses on all individual participants. Using conventional polymerase chain reaction (PCR) amplification of DNA through exon 3 makes it challenging to distinguish between MWS and LWS gene sequences at codon 180. This is because of the 98% nucleotide sequence identity between the MWS and LWS opsin genes. The method we use here is a combination of molecular methods to enable accurate genotyping at exon 3, codon 180 for both the MWS and LWS genes, and other exons. The method draws from the published work of Winderickx et al., Neitz and Neitz and colleagues, Asenjo et al., and Sharpe et al. In particular, the method is similar to one described by Winderickx et al. (1992), but differs in that it incorporates an additional confirmation of exon 4 and 5 gene-specific amino acids sequences. This additional confirmation is based on descriptions given by Asenjo et al. (1994) and Sharpe et al. (1998), which together distinguish the genomic regions of DNA sequence variation between MWS and LWS genes (Neitz et al. 1991, 1995; Winderickx et al. 1992; Asenjo et al. 1994; Sharpe et al. 1998).

The present genotyping procedures expand on earlier methods described by Wasserman, Szeszel, and Jameson (2009) for the isolation of the L-180-serine/alanine polymorphism, and the genetic research just cited provides the empirical justification for these genotyping methods. In short, the present method uses a combination of three molecular approaches first to create MWS and LWS gene-specific DNA templates, and then uses those templates to distinguish between their respective codon 180 sequences. A long-range polymerase chain reaction technique (LR PCR) generates gene-specific PCR products. DNA sequencing of each PCR template confirms this gene specificity, and determines MWS and LWS codon 180 genotypes. The method enables accurate genotyping of the codon 180 polymorphism on each photopigment opsin gene. Thus, fine comparisons can be made between genotype and color matching behavior. Analyses using this method demonstrate a close correlation with perceptual behavior and provide significant insight into mechanisms contributing to the variability in perceptual behavior. Detail of the genotyping procedures used is described in Atilano et al. (2020).

3.1.2 Why Investigate the L-180 Cone Locus for Tetrachromacy?

Early investigations, beginning with those of Nagy et al. (1981), located potential tetrachromat genotypes by identifying women with impaired color vision relatives. Subsequent advances that clarified gene sequence variation now give additional understanding of the genetic events that can create hybrid and fusion gene configurations, and the ways recombined genes are associated with relatively large separations between expressed photopigment variants of some potential tetrachromats (e.g., the cDA29 participant of Jordan et al. 2010).

Some potential tetrachromats, such as cDA29, exhibit genotypes that are rare and difficult to find because they are composed of recombined gene segments, possibly including multiple, and infrequent, SNPs. In such cases multiple SNPs can additively contribute to shifts in photopigment spectral sensitivity and produce uncommon phenotype configurations that are, because of the photo-receptor response profiles they produce, especially good candidates for tetrachromacy.

L-180-Serine/Alanine SNP Variants Are Frequently Occurring. A more common form of color vision genetic variation found in people of European ancestry is the allelic variations due to a *single-nucleotide polymorphism* (SNP) found at exon 3 of the L-opsin at codon 180. This L-180-serine/alanine variant occurs in Caucasians at about 60%/40% frequency, respectively, and for this reason it has been widely studied because of the increased likelihood of finding large numbers of females possessing both allelic variants. In addition, not only does the relatively similar frequency of allelic variants in the population mean the chance of finding a female L-180 heterozygote is good, but the search for such heterzygotes can also be guided by surveying females with male relatives who have an X-linked color vision deficiency such as anomalous trichromacy.

L-180-Serine/Alanine Heterozygosity Produces L-Cone Variants with Sufficiently Separated Peak Spectral Sensitivities. While both L-180-ser-ine/alanine forms are commonly occurring alleles, the trade-off in the pheno-type is that the spectral shifts of expressed photopigments produced by the L-180 variants are smaller (at about a 4–5 nm spread) than, for example, the shifts that can arise from heterozygosities on the L-opsin's exon 5's 277 or 285 loci. Even so, despite the relatively minor spectral difference of the L-180 variants compared to those that can potentially arise from heterozygosities at other loci, individuals possessing both L-180 variants are relatively easy to find, and for this reason L-180 is considered a sensible SNP locus for inves-tigation. Moreover, an argument can be made that finding even a moderate perceptual consequence under a lesser spectral shift would be an important empirical result, because it would demonstrate the utility of signals provided by a fourth class of photoreceptor, and it would thereby support the remark-able idea that a form of tetrachromat functionality can indeed be realized by enlisting a richer neural color code. It is also plausible that possession of both L-180 SNP variants might underlie non-normative perceptual variation if one considers that the substantial difference in perceptual experience attributable to the M-cone and L-cone peak response sensitivities is due to a separation of about 30 nm.s between response peaks. In light of this, it is reasonable to expect that a 4–5-nm spectral separation should, at a minimum, produce qualitatively different red and orange-red sensations, and that such a difference should be observable empirically. Indeed, research suggests peak sensitivity separations even on the order of 1–2 nm are sufficient to impact perceptual matches (Crognale et al. 1998; Thomas et al. 2011). Thus, there is good reason to suppose that signals from an L-180-serine/alanine phenotype are sufficient to contribute to the development of neural processing mechanisms that could support functional tetrachromacy (MacLeod and von der Twer 2003).

L-180-Serine/Alanine Variants Have Been Previously Studied and Their Features Are Understood. Much genetics and color vision research has focused on the perceptual correlates of this common X-chromosome-linked, exon 3, L-180 opsin gene polymorphism. As mentioned, in some populations the L-180 opsin gene amino acid residues can alternatively be either serine or alanine. L-180 SNP variants have been shown to underlie variable sensitivity to long-wavelength stimuli, with the serine variant's maximal sensitivity peak at longer wavelengths compared to that of the alanine variant (Deeb 2005). Changes in spectral tuning of photopigment sensitivity peak attributable to L-180 amino acid residues have also linked the L-180 polymorphism to individual variations in normal color vision. (Deeb 2004; Neitz and Neitz 2011; Gardner et al. 2014).

As mentioned, due to the X-chromosome-linked inheritance of both the MWS and LWS photopigment opsin genes, individuals with two X chromosomes can be heterozygous (inheriting one variant from the maternal X and the other variant from the paternal X) and as a result carry and express two different allelic variants of M- or L-opsin genes. This nondeleterious heterozygosity can arise from a simple nucleotide substitution at a single genetic locus, abbreviated "SNP" for single nucleotide polymorphism, or it can occur as a consequence of multiple nucleotide substitutions. The L-180 heterozygosity is often found in female carriers of color vision anomalies.

Knowledge about the frequency of occurrence of the L-180 opsin heterozygosity, along with data suggesting its nontrivial impact on color vision processing (seen, for example, in anomalous trichromat male individuals), has led to the systematic investigation of carriers of L-180 heterozygosities as a possible genetic indicator for potential color vision tetrachromacy. Research finds the L-180 polymorphism (similar to amino acid polymorphisms at L-opsin positions 277 and 285) to be associated with perceptual processing differences for some candidate tetrachromats (Sanocki et al. 1994; Crognale et al. 1998;

Jameson et al. 1998a, 1998b, 2001, 2006, 2015, 2016, 2018; Bimler et al. 2004; Deeb 2005; Sayim et al. 2005; Jordan et al. 2010; Bochko et al. 2017; Bochko and Jameson 2018).

Figure 2a depicts an L-180-serine form of trichromat genotype showing the presence of a single L-cone opsin gene variant. By comparison Figure 2b illustrates a potential tetrachromat genotype, with dashed and solid arrows indicating presence of two L-cone opsin gene variants (L-180-serine and L-180-alanine, respectively). While SNP variations at a number of other possible gene sequence loci can also provide for potential tetrachromacy, evaluating this particular L-opsin genetic variant as a basis for potential tetrachromacy builds upon our previous research investigating individuals heterozygous for the L-180 polymorphism at exon 3 (Jameson et al. 1998a, 1998b, 2001, 2006, 2015, 2016, 2018; Bimler et al. 2004; Sayim et al. 2005; Bochko and Bochko et al. 2017; Jameson 2018). The present study goes beyond our previous work, however, in that we assess all participants' full opsin genotype (rhodopsin, S-, M-, and L-opsins), which is discussed in the text that follows to explore additional impacts on perceptual processing that can arise from sequence variations at genetic loci other than L-180.

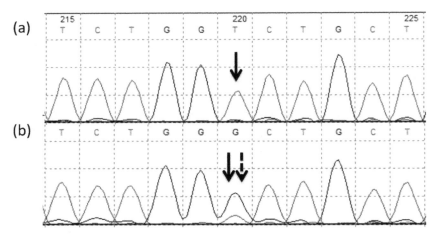

Figure 2 Chromatograms depicting sequence analysis results for long-wavelength-sensitive (LWS) cone photopigment opsin genes. Arrows indicate alleles present at a specific locus of the L-opsin, exon 3, at codon 180. In (a) a single solid arrow shows detection of an allelic variant associated with trichromat genotypes. In (b) the dashed and solid arrows show the presence of two allelic variants underlying some potential tetrachromat genotypes. Full opsin genotyping (including rhodopsin, S-, M-, and L-opsins) was conducted on all participants and is reported elsewhere.

3.2 Methods and Design

The present experiments assessed accuracy of color matches to target samples in a novel color reproduction task. Table 1 lists the 10 volunteers who participated in three experiments, showing their age, genetic sequences for retinal photopigments, gender, and artistic training. A total of 41 Munsell Color System singleton colors were randomly presented, and participants were tasked with accurately reproducing each target color on an adjacent blank canvas using oil paint pigment mixtures from a standard palette. The experiments were conducted under three different illumination conditions to assess within-participant robustness of matching performance across varying chromatic adaptation states. Appendix Figure A1 shows spectral power distribution of one of the illumination conditions tested, namely that using the D65 approximate illuminant.

3.2.1 Rationale for the Color Reproduction Task

A color reproduction task was used to assess individual variation in color perception. The task was previously shown to be a useful investigative approach for observers who have substantial color training and expertise, presumably because they are accomplished painters with high-level skills in reproducing perceived color using paints on canvas (Bochko et al. 2017; Bochko and Jameson 2018). The present study included both professional artists and nonartist participants. Identical color reproduction task instructions were given to

Table 1 Ten participants' demographics

ID #	Age	L-180 allele serine (S) alanine (A)	Sex	Color assessment	Artist/ nonartist
01	54	S	M	Average	Artist
02	53	A and S	F	Superior	Nonartist
03	26	A and S	F	Superior	Artist
04	20	S	F	Superior	Nonartist
05	21	A	F	Superior	Artist
06	54	A and S	F	Superior	Artist
07	30	S	F	Superior	Nonartist
08	32	A	M	Dichromat	Nonartist
09	23	A	M	Average	Nonartist
10	27	S	M	Superior	Nonartist

all participants, emphasizing that they were to "take as much time as needed to exactly duplicate the color shown (the Munsell color chip target stimuli) using the pigment palette provided, paying the utmost attention to color reproduction accuracy," permitting participants to " . . . adjust any one of the color patches at any time . . . " before signaling to the experimenter that they either (1) achieved an identical, or the best possible, color match between a sample and its reproduction, or (2) were unable to achieve a satisfactory color match using the pigment palette provided (for further details see Bochko and Jameson 2018). Participants were asked to rate their subjective accuracy of each match produced on a rating scale where a rating of "1" indicated "a failure to match" and "9" indicated "a perfect match."

Our design of this color reproduction task is based on two assumptions. First, satisfactory matches can be achieved by both artists and nonartists; and, second, to the extent each observer can accurately reproduce the appearance of a target color stimuli with a pigment mixture, it was expected that comparing goodness-of-fit across participants' matches relative to those predicted by a standard observer model would provide useful information on color perception variations across individual participants. Both these assumptions are evaluated in data analyses presented in the text that follows.

Following the designs of our earlier studies (Jameson et al. 2016; Bochko and Bockho et al. 2017; Jameson 2018) each individual research participant completed five experimental blocks during a single experimental session, which ranged between approximately 4.5 and 6 hours duration. All sessions included (1) task instructions and informed consent for all experiment tasks; (2) standardized assessment of participants' color perception; (3) collection of participants' DNA specimens for subsequent photopigment opsin genotyping; (4) completing the color reproduction task under three different adaptation conditions (duration of each condition individually varied between approximately 35 and 90 minutes); and (5) postexperiment debriefing.

3.2.2 Participants

The 10 participants listed in Table 1 included "artists" ($N = 4$; #01, #03, #05, #06), three of these were females; and "nonartists" ($N = 6$; #02, #04, #07, #08, #09, #10) three were females. Participants' ages ranged between 20 and 54 years. Participants provided informed written consent using procedures adhering to protocols compliant with the World Medical Association declaration of Helsinki ethical principles for research involving human subjects. All research protocols were approved by the ethical review board of the University of California, Irvine (UCI IRB#2003–3131, IRB#1993–0093).

3.2.3 Retinal Opsin Genotyping

Participants volunteered to provide venous blood or saliva specimens (or both) for opsin genotyping (Atilano et al. 2017, 2020). Participant DNA was extracted and analyzed using verified PCR techniques (based on novel procedures described in Atilano et al. 2017, 2020, which improves upon existing methods of Wasserman et al. 2009) and sequencing procedures for isolation of opsin gene sequence information and for the full complement of standard visual pigments including rhodopsin, short- (S-), medium- (M-), and long- (L-) wavelength-sensitive photopigments and their allelic variants (Jameson et al. 2001; Wasserman et al. 2009; Atilano et al. 2017). Figure 2 depicts an excerpt of gene sequencing results for L-photopigment opsin gene regions on exon 3, at codon 180 of the L-cone opsin gene (or L-180-serine/alanine).

3.2.4 Assessment of Color Perception

All participants had normal or corrected-to-normal visual acuity. Their color vision was assessed using standardized tools including the Ishihara Pseudo-isochromatic Plates (Ishihara 1994), and the Farnsworth–Munsell 100-hue Test (Farnsworth 1949, revised 1957). In the present study small field anomaloscope matches were not assessed owing to their presumed limited utility as an informative index of the detailed impacts of retinal tetrachromacy, and the preferred anomaloscope matching equipment – large field center-surround anomaloscope matching – was not available for use in the present study. As seen in Table 1, on the color vision assessment tests used all participants were classified as having normal or superior color vision, apart from one dichromat (participant #08) with deuteranopia due to M-cone deficiency.

3.2.5 Color Reproduction Task Stimuli and Procedure

Experimental Stimuli. Figure 3a illustrates the color reproduction task, employing an oil paint pigment palette comprised of specifically chosen colors, as described in Bochko and Jameson (2018). Table 2 lists the pigments and the product manufacturer. This task assesses the degree to which individual's painted reproductions matched both the subjective appearance and the measured reflectance spectra of color target stimuli under a D65-approximate illuminant.

Figure 4 shows the approximate color appearance of each of 18 pure pigments used in the palette. Statistical analyses of measured palette spectra

Table 2 Eighteen oil paint pigments used to create the standardized palette employed in all experiments (shown in Figure 3)

1	Yellow Ochre #744
2	Burnt Sienna #74
3	Burnt Umber #76
4	Raw Umber #554
5	Raw Sienna #552
6	Permanent Alizarin Crimson #468
7	Viridian Hue #696
8	Cobalt Blue #178
9	French Ultramarine #263
10	Cerulean Blue Hue #138
11	Permanent Rose #502
12	Dioxazine Purple #229
13	Windsor Emerald #708
14	Cadmium Yellow Pale Hue #119
15	Cadmium Red Light #100
16	Permanent Green Light #483
17	Cadmium Orange #89
18	Titanium White #644

Winsor and Newton, Winton Oil Colour Series 1. www.winsornewton.com

determined that the reflectance spectra of the 18-pigment palette employed was adequate for participants to reproduce the reflectance spectra of the target stimuli by palette pigment mixtures (see Appendix for details).

An important feature of this investigation compared to previous research is that we sought to use a relatively large number of stimuli that widely sample from a representative range of color appearance space regions. The target stimuli were 41 surface color samples that widely sampled most salient categorical regions of color appearance space; and all colors were characterized as both surface reflectance spectra and in Munsell Color System notation. Specifically, the 41-item stimulus set included 24 samples from the Macbeth ColorChecker (MCC) calibration standard (2014), which are representative of several perceptual color space categories and dimensions and, importantly, are also based on an underlying mainstream theory of standard normal color perception, and are therefore widely considered acceptable for use as a standardized stimulus in color vision research (colors depicted in Figure 5).

In addition, 17 stimuli from the Munsell Book of Color (Matte Edition) were used (Munsell 1976). The 17 Munsell stimuli were chosen using a

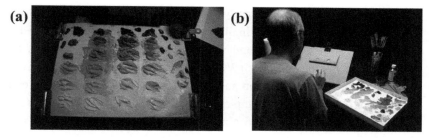

Figure 3 A color reproduction task required participants to create pigment palette mixtures and reproduce, on a blank canvas, color appearance matches for 41 target color stimuli under a D65 approximate illuminant. (a) The standardized pigment palette used by all participants, detailed elsewhere (Bochko and Jameson 2018). Briefly, the palette comprised 18 unique pools of oil paint pigments and 16 additive mixtures of white pigment blended with one of four pigment primaries (reddish, greenish, yellowish, and bluish pigments) from among the 18 pigments employed. Thus, the palette consisted of 18 unique pigments for use, and 16 premixed pools of pigment-plus-white. Figure 4 lists the 18 unique pigments used. (b) A participant engaged in the color reproduction task with a lavender-hue color target stimulus shown as the left-hand circular color and an in-progress color reproduction match shown in the right-hand position of the color pair. The color reproduction task was self-paced, and each experiment was typically completed in 60–80 minutes.

principled empirically-based image filtering approach that was derived from independent psychophysical data (see Jameson et al. 2015, 2016). As detailed in Jameson et al. (2015, 2016), selection of the 17 Munsell colors was based on a process that used a filtering algorithm designed to identify salient colors from the pixels of images and photographs for which two observers' perceptions differed.

Briefly, the filter algorithm was designed to identify from within an image the pixel-wise processed spectral reflectances that were predicted to significantly vary across nondeficient observers. This is achieved through image processing results of pixel-wise reflectance spectra procedures using first a filter based on an empirical model of color perception from an L-180 potential tetrachromat (specifically participant #06), which was then compared to a second perceptual filter defined by the empirical results from normal color vision trichromat observers. Comparing these observer-based filtering approaches permitted identification of a subset of Munsell Book of Color stimuli that a trichromat and a tetrachromat would

be expected to perceive differently. That is, to objectively find a reason-
ably sized subset of Munsell stimuli, our filtering algorithm was applied to
the image of a well-known standard Munsell color stimulus, namely, the
330-color World Color Survey (WCS) stimulus set widely used in investigations of color categorization and naming (see www1.icsi.berkeley.edu/
wcs/grid.jpg). Applying our empirical filter to all 330 Munsell colors in
the WCS stimulus grid yielded a result of 17 Munsell samples shown in
Figure 6 (from among the set of 330 considered) as those that would be
perceived in a significantly variable way by our L-180 heterozygote model
compared to a normal trichromat observer model.

Experimental Procedure. The aim of the color reproduction task was to have
participants use their desired combination of color palette pigment mixtures to
individually obtain their best achievable color appearance match to stimuli
from a set that widely sampled from salient categorical regions of color
appearance space. Note that the present study's assessment of 41 color stimulus matches represents a substantially larger set than that typically found in
psychophysical investigations on tetrachromacy and is thereby more probative of perceptual color space than stimulus sets previously used in previous
investigations.

All experiments involved presentation of 41 color stimuli in a target-match
sample pair consisting of a singleton 1-inch circular target color stimulus
adjacent to a 1-inch circular blank white canvas, both presented mounted in a
neutral achromatic gray holder (Munsell gray = $N/6.5$). Figure 3b depicts a
participant in the experimental booth completing the task, where the target is
mounted on the left, and a blank circular canvas, which the participant was
required to paint to match the color of the target, is on the right. Using this
format, large-field (>6.0 degrees) color matches were obtained, as viewing
distance in trials was unconstrained and freely varied between 10 and 17 inches
distant from the surface of presented stimuli. Typically each 1-inch stimulus
subtended a minimum of 6 degrees of visual angle, with the pair of circles
subtending approximately 17 degrees visual angle.

The 41 color reproduction trials, as shown in Figure 3b, were presented to
all participants one at a time in the same fixed random order. The task was
self-paced and participants were allowed as much time as they needed to use
the pigment palette as instructed to "exactly duplicate the target colors shown
at left on the blank white canvas at right while ... paying utmost attention
to color reproduction accuracy ... ". While duration of the sessions tended
to be longer for those participants who did not have artistic training, all
participants (professional artists and nonartists alike) completed the task

with relative ease and with a noticeable degree of enthusiasm. Further methodological details are presented elsewhere (Bochko and Jameson 2018; Jameson et al. 2018).

3.3 Results

3.3.1 Color Spectral Reflectance Measurements

Similar to methods detailed by Bochko and Jameson (2018), participants' color reproduction performance was assessed using spectrophotometric measurements of both the target stimuli and the empirically generated reproductions. A standardized protocol was applied across participants and conditions to ensure measurement accuracy and permit repeated-measure verification. An Ocean Optics USB Flame spectrometer interfaced with custom spectral power distribution scripts (Mathematica V. 9.0.4) was used to measure and quantify each participant's color reproductions; to verify repeated measures for all target stimuli; and establish accuracy of observed spectral power distribution data through analyses of spectral reflectance measurements.

Figure 4 presents results from analyses that characterize the error inherent in the measured reflectance spectra of the palette pigments when wet (i.e., as when participants were carrying out, judging, and completing their matching performance during the experiment) and when dry (i.e., days after the experimental session when the oil painted matches were dry and when spectral reflectance measurements were done to construct datasets for analyses). Our analyses found the variation in measurement across wet and dry pigment pairs generally conformed to tolerance limits empirically identified by assessing repeated measure error. Thus, the surface reflectance measurements of match samples when dry can be taken to be comparable to those the subject evaluated during the experiment when the oil paints of match samples were still wet.

Figures 5 and 6 show reflectance spectra measures plotted for 41 target stimuli. Figure 5 depicts measures for the 24 colors from the Macbeth ColorChecker (MCC) calibration standard. Figure 6 provides measures for the 17 additional Munsell Book of Color samples used.

In summary, the present results suggest findings that accord with those of our earlier research that used a color reproduction task variation (Jameson et al. 2018). Briefly, the present study reveals two important findings: First, all 10 participants were able to accomplish personally acceptable pigment mixtures in the required color reproduction task. Second, the accuracy of participants' color reproductions was systematically impacted by (1) the degree of the

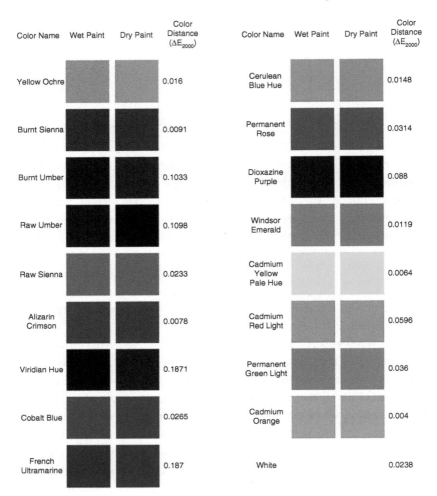

Figure 4 Colorimetric measures and computationally approximated color appearances of wet and dry oil pigments used in the experimental palette employed. Color names listed in column 1 correspond to the Winsor and Newton, Winton Oil Colour Series 1 names provided in Table 2. Columns 2 and 3 provide approximations of computed color appearances of wet and dry pigments, respectively. Based on measures of reflectance spectra from wet palette samples and corresponding measures of samples once dry, we obtained wet/dry subjective color differences as represented in the column showing ΔE (2000) values, derived using CIEDE2000 color-difference formula based on the CIELAB color space (Luo et al. 2001).

participant's artistic training, (2) the individual's photopigment opsin geno-type, and (3) the spectral composition of the illuminants under which stimuli were viewed and reproductions were painted.

Additional findings were realized using approaches introduced by Bochko and Jameson (2018). These include genetic algorithm modeling and nonnega-tive matrix factorization data analyses that when applied to individual data revealed insights concerning the nonuniformity and dimensionality of partici-pants' color reproduction spaces. In the text that follows we detail some of these results.

3.3.2 Opsin Genotyping Results

Participants' DNA sequences for retinal photopigment opsin genes were assessed and found to represent varied opsin genotypes. Table 1, column 3, provides the genotyping results relevant for the present investigation. Three participants (IDs #02, #03, and #06) exhibit the SNP of interest, namely, L-180-serine/alanine opsin heterozygosity at codon 180 of exon 3. These three participants possess genes for expressing an extra L-cone variant in their retinae, implying they have a particular form of potential tetrachromat phenotype. Seven of the participants (IDs #01, #04, #05, #07, #08, #09 and #10) possess only one of two possible L-180 cone opsin allelic variants, implying normal trichromat color vision genotypes with respect to L-cone variation. In addition to L-cone opsin genotype data, analyses of M-cone opsin sequences for participants indicated an M-cone opsin gene was not detected for one participant (#08); thus, as standardized color vision assessment confirms, this participant is perceptually a deuter-anope (or green color deficient) due to an absence of a normal M-cone opsin gene sequence. All other participants exhibited at least one full M-cone gene variant.

Thus, the present sample of 10 participants includes one verified deuter-anope dichromat male, 6 verified normal color vision participants with tri-chromat genotypes (4 of L-180-serine variant and 2 of L-180-alanine variant), and 3 verified color vision normal females who are heterozygous for L-opsin variants and who are therefore candidate tetrachromats. Additional genotyp-ing results for S-opsin and rhodopsin for the 10 participants are available but are not reported here because they are not crucial for interpreting the color reproduction task findings discussed.

As mentioned earlier, Table 1 allows evaluation of participants' data in relation to their color training expertise: some of them (#01, #03, #05 and #06) are professional artists who presumably are more experienced in making

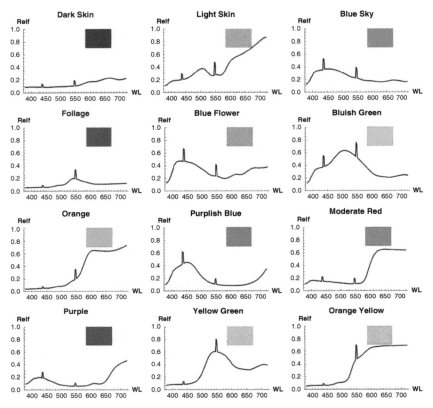

Figure 5 Surface reflectance measurement plots for 24 experimental stimuli from the Macbeth ColorChecker (1976) illuminated by D65 approximate shown in Figure A1. Approximate color appearances (sRGB) of reflectances are shown as inset panels. Color checker names are shown as panel titles. Spikes in stimulus reflectance spectra are an inherent feature of the fluorescent tube illuminant of the D65 source used, as shown in Figure A1 in the Appendix.

color matches with paint pigment mixtures, and who likely have expertise in the domain of conceptualizing color appearance matches between surface colors and palette mixtures. This aspect of our participant group is considered in the analyses that follow.

3.3.3 Color Reproduction Task Results

For the present report three hypotheses – enumerated (i)–(iii) in Section 3.3.3.1 – were addressed to describe the relationships between participants'

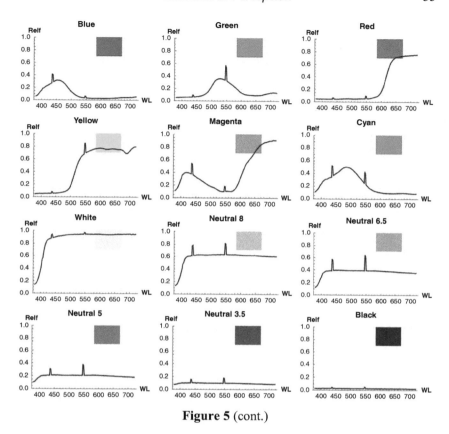

Figure 5 (cont.)

abilities to match the target stimuli in the color reproduction task and the individually varying factors expected to impact color perception. Factors considered include (1) photopigment opsin genotype, (2) perceptual expertise achieved by artistic training, (3) gender, and (4) color vision performance in typically employed standardized color vision testing. Hypotheses (i) to (iii) related to these factors are detailed in Section 3.3.3.1.

3.3.3.1 Spatial Representation and Quantified Accuracy of Participants' Color Reproductions in Terms of Two Colorimetric Spaces

We used the target and painted reproductions spectral reflectance measurements to quantify the observed color space differences for each individual's pairwise color reproduction performance. This allowed us to measure the degree to which participants were able to produce color matches. This was done for each participant by using two metric frameworks to quantify

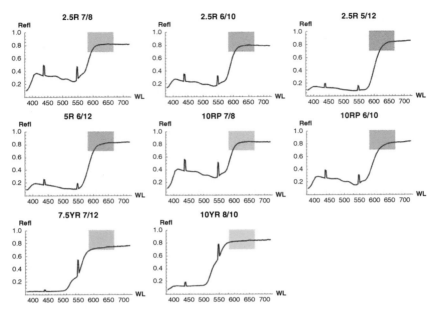

Figure 6 Surface reflectance measurement plots for 17 experimental stimuli from the Munsell Book of Color (1976) illuminated by D65 approximate shown in Figure A1. Approximate color appearances (sRGB) of reflectances are shown as panel insets. Munsell Hue Value/Chroma (H V/C) notations are shown as panel titles. Spikes in stimulus reflectance spectra are an inherent feature of the fluorescent tube illuminant of the D65 source used, as shown in Figure A1 in the Appendix.

measured color differences for all 41 target-to-match-sample pairs. First, we employed a rigorous embedding of color reproduction distances in a Munsell metric space to compare nonparametric Euclidean distances between each pair of measured targets and reproduced colors when embedded in Munsell Color Space. Using this method allows rigorous quantification of an individual's reproduction errors as Euclidean metric distances (Satalich 2015). Second, we used a well-known color difference index, CIE ΔE ($L*u*v*$), from a standard tristimulus color space (Smith and Guild 1931; Luo et al. 2001; Schanda 2007). While method (1) is flexible with respect to the underlying observer model assumed and can be made nonparametric, method (2) permits assessment of color matching under the assumption of well-known CIE standard observer theory.

By quantifying target and color-match differences in color space using measured reflectance spectra, we can evaluate hypotheses (i) and (ii): Namely, (i) individuals with color processing expertise (such as artists) are expected to exhibit reduced color reproduction error compared to age- and gender-matched

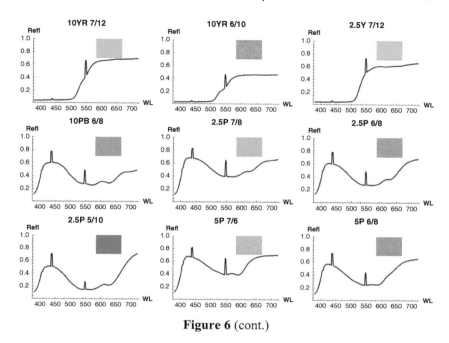

Figure 6 (cont.)

nonartists (e.g., results of Figures 7 and 8). And (ii) individuals with color vision phenotypes that could confer color processing advantages (such as potential tetrachromats) might exhibit a reduced degree of color reproduction error compared to age- and gender-matched standard normal trichromat observers, especially compared to dichromats (e.g., results of Figures 7 and 8). And, a hypothesis that is clarified just below and by detail provided in Section 3.3.3.4 is (iii): Regardless of color processing expertise, age, or gender, color reproduction error variation should be associated with confusion regions of perceptual color space that can be predicted from opsin genotyping (e.g., results of Figures 7, 8, 9 and 10).

The logic behind (iii) is initially made clear by considering some examples. First, suppose in our surface color-matching experiment we assess dichromat participants who possess opsin genotypes that are lacking either an M- or L-opsin gene. Such dichromats would be expected to empirically exhibit greater-than-normal color reproduction error in color space regions delimited by confusion lines typically associated with the identified photopigment defect. Thus, an M-cone or deutan dichromat (e.g., participant 8 here) is expected to have high reproduction errors for certain stimuli, especially for colors within a particular green-to-yellow-to-red stimulus range. In addition, a protanope participant with an L-cone deficit would be expected to have relatively large color matching errors in orange and reddish regions of color space. Other individual forms of varying color reproduction error (albeit less severe than those of a dichromat) can also be modeled and predicted from opsin gene sequence variations (e.g., due to SNPs at loci 180, 277, and 285) that additively combine to shift expressed MWS- and LWS-photopigment peaks closer to one another. Such cases reflect the rough gradient of possible anomalous trichromat observer variants that have predictable color matching error patterns which are associated with varying photopigment peak response properties, which furthermore are attributable to opsin genotype sequences.

Extending the foregoing reasoning, it should also be true that some relative *decreases* in color reproduction error are to be expected for potential tetrachromats, and such error reductions should be especially evident when participants are matching color appearances that enlist those cone response features provided by a specific four-photopigment cone model that is expressed by a particular candidate tetrachromat genotype under consideration. Thus, to the degree that genetically-based tetrachromat perceptual variation exists, and can be empirically measured along the dimensions present in the space of color appearance stimuli we employ here, the empirical demonstration of reduced tetrachromat color reproduction errors (relative to the observed magnitudes of normal color observer errors) might demand only a sufficiently granular degree of stimulus variation to isolate the color processing differences that occur along color space axes of individual L-180-serine/alanine tetrachromat processing (i.e., modeled in Figure 1b).

In this way opsin genotype sequences can be used to model individual participants' cone responses to spectra, which in turn can be used to predict color matching performance variation across color space, and which then can be compared across individual observers with different underlying genotypes. Results presented below use this approach to investigate color perception variations that arise from different limiting conditions present in individual's retinas.

3.3.3.2 Results on Participants' Color Reproduction Accuracy.

Following the aforementioned rationale, empirical results from the D65 illumination condition are depicted in Figure 7. For each participant Figure 7 shows dyads of the measured reflectance spectra of 41 targets plotted in Munsell Color Space paired with corresponding points from measures of empirically reproduced color spectra. Dyads with very similar reflectance spectra are plotted near each other in color space, and reproduction error magnitude is represented by a given dyad's connecting line segment length in metric Euclidean distances.

Figure 7 shows that the target-to-match-sample error differences (indicated by connecting line segments), and the insets of average error values, imply that the surface color reproduction task is a useful empirical procedure for capturing subjective color matching. We also see there is good reproduction accuracy across most participants – the exceptions being one dichromat participant (#08) and one trichromat male participant (#10) both discussed in the text that follows in the context of Figure 8. Second, average reproduction errors also suggest that female participants generally show smaller target-to-match-sample errors than male participants (with the exception being one female potential tetrachromat artist, participant #03, exhibiting error values comparable to those of two nonartist trichromat males, #09 and #10).

Further, as expected, the dichromat's (#08) average reproduction error indicates the least accurate color reproduction performance, which is impaired in ways predicted by a deuteranope confusion axis in the red–green direction of color space. Finally, Figure 7 also suggests that embedding color reproduction task outcomes using the metric of the Munsell Color Space provides a useful tool for birds-eye insights into the role of such factors as gender and individual variation in color vision phenotype among our participants. This type of analysis also enables insight into the role of color *expertise* in artists, who exhibit smaller color reproduction error compared to nonartist participants.

3.3.3.3 Differentiating Potential Tetrachromat from Trichromat Performance

The precise manner with which color reproduction results in Figure 7 distinguish potential tetrachromat participants from normal trichromat participants initially seems less than obvious. This is perhaps not surprising, as Figure 7 shows results for all 41 experimental stimuli across the entire color space and, based on photopigment variation alone, it seems unlikely that a tetrachromat observer would necessarily exhibit color perception differences across all portions of the color space. What is more plausible, given the analysis rationale detailed earlier, is that a potential tetrachromat who exhibits nonnormative color perception variation should exhibit variation in regions of color space that relate to color processes associated with the expression of the specific extra photopigment variant they possess. Thus, to appreciate the differences found for a potential tetrachromat it is crucial to examine the specific subsets of our 41 stimuli that are predicted to differ for the form of L-180 heterozygote studied here, and this is achieved by specifically examining where L-180 color processing variation might be expected given an assumption of color perception under a D65 illuminant model (Jameson et al. 2015, 2016).

(a) Potential Tetrachromat (#02)

$\mu(D) = 0.088$

(b) Potential Tetrachromat (#03)

$\mu(D) = 0.132$　　　　　　Artist

(c) Potential Tetrachromat (#06)

$\mu(D) = 0.073$　　　　Artist

(d) Trichromat male (#01)

$\mu(D) = 0.087$　　Artist

(e) Trichromat female (#04)

$\mu(D) = 0.093$

(f) Trichromat female (#05)

$\mu(D) = 0.089$　　　　Artist

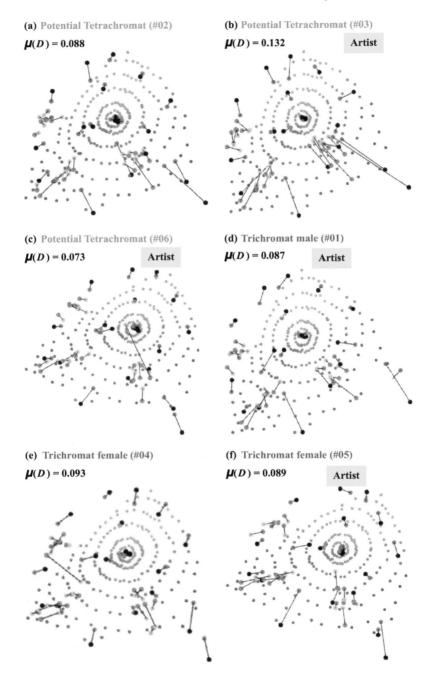

(g) Trichromat female (#07)

$\mu(D) = 0.063$

(h) Trichromat male (#09)

$\mu(D) = 0.132$

(i) Trichromat male (#10)

$\mu(D) = 0.135$

(j) Dichromat male (#08)

$\mu(D) = 0.217$

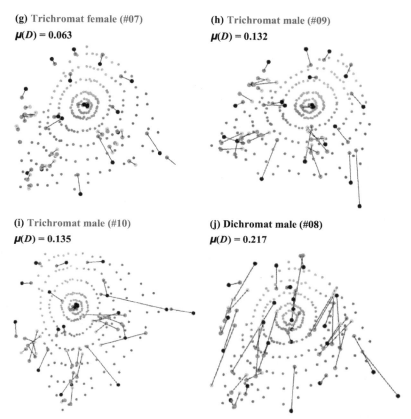

Figure 7 Spatial representation plots of reflectance measurements for all stimuli and pigment-match samples from 10 participants (plots a–j). Plots (a)–(c) are individual potential tetrachromat data, plots (d)–(i) show trichromats, and plot (j) shows a dichromat. Artist participants are (b), (c), (d), and (f). Each plot presents all 41 target stimuli, with each individual's 41 corresponding pigment matches, embedded in the Value = 5 plane of the space defined by the Munsell Book of Color (1976). Line segments that connect two displayed points represent Euclidean distances that quantify the error found in a participant's reproduction. The 24 Macbeth ColorChecker stimulus targets are represented as black dots, and corresponding pigment-matches are shown as gray dots. The 17 Munsell color stimulus targets are represented as red dots, and corresponding pigment matches are shown as pink dots. An index of each participant's average error in the task is computed as the observed mean line segment Euclidean distance, or μ(D).

3.3.3.4 Spatial Representation and Quantification of Color Reproduction Accuracy in CIELUV Space for Colors Identified as Salient Using a Tetrachromat Filter Algorithm

Thus, to explore the potential tetrachromat effect in greater detail, we next chose to narrow our examination of color space, and used Gaussian mixture model machine learning procedures to locate for each participant's data the best fitting ellipses in CIELUV space for three sets of target-match-to-sample pairs – namely, the reddish, yellowish, and lavender sets shown in Figure 6. Recall that stimuli shown in Figure 6 are predicted by empirical filter analyses to be processed differently by the studied form of L-180 potential tetrachromat compared to a trichromat (Jameson et al. 2016). Results of this analysis for each participant are presented in CIELUV space in Figure 8. Each panel shows three pairs of ellipses – a pair of ellipses fit to six stimuli of reddish color (Figure 6, panels 1–6), one pair of ellipses fit to five stimuli of yellowish color (Figure 6, panels 7–11), and one pair of ellipses fit to six stimuli of lavender color (Figure 6, panels 12–17). To complement the Guassian mixture model solutions, computed ΔE color differences (based on the CIE modeled reflectance measures of each participant's match-to-target performance) are also provided as inset $\mu(\Delta E(L * u * v *))$ values. The provided color difference measures convey each individual's overall average reproduction error found for Figure 6's 17 Munsell Book of Color stimuli.

Pairs of estimated ellipses in each case include a blue ellipse (representing the ellipse fit to a participant's color match measures) and a black ellipse (representing the ellipse fit to target stimulus measures). The degree of overlap between the black and blue ellipse pairs indicates the degree of estimated concordance between target stimulus measures relative to measures of empirically observed matches. Visual consideration of ellipse correspondence detail suggests the results closely follow the filter predictions for potential tetrachromats. For example, as predicted previously (in Jameson et al. [2016] and by algorithmic filter identification of the stimuli in Figure 6), the correspondence of the black and blue ellipse pairs for the reddish and yellowish sets of stimuli is more closely aligned for potential tetrachromat participants compared to normal trichromat participants, *and* the correspondence of ellipse pairs for the lavender set is by comparison more misaligned for tetrachromats than that seen across the normal trichromats we tested. These countervailing predictions – facilitated matching for some colors, attenuated matching for others – were made by a filter algorithm that is based on independent psychophysical data from a confirmed L-180 tetrachromat (Jameson et al. 2016). The fact that both predictions are confirmed in the current tetrachromat study (using a very different surface color perception task) lends confidence to the perceptual matching variation found for our present tetrachromat participants and underscores the relevance of the specific color space regions examined here, for which tetrachromat variation is demonstrated.

Confidence in this interpretation also comes from the fact that the ellipse results are congruent with the plausible consequences one would predict from the presumed operating characteristics of the chromatic response functions associated with a heterozygous L-180 photopigment opsin profile (cf. Figure 1b). In other words, the spectral regions where the L-180 tetrachromat cone function sensitivities are expected to deviate from normal trichromat cone responses were found to be consistent with the color appearance regions where performance variations were found in both (1) the initial psychophysical results (Jameson et al. 2016) and (2) the error measures we observe for individuals' matches in the present pigment color reproduction task. Moreover, observed tetrachromat impacts that resemble local variation (as opposed to global variation) in color space were previously suggested by our tetrachromat filter predictions and accord with our earlier suggestion that some form of color processing "bias" seems likely. That is, observed variation in processing across color appearance regions shows that for some color regions perceptual processing improves relative to that shown for normal trichromat processing, whereas for other regions color processing is attenuated relative to a trichromat norm. A feature of variable perceptual processing for specific predictable areas of color appearance space is analogous to predictable dichromat processing differences and might be an empirical characteristic of human tetrachromat phenotypes that has not been sufficiently investigated in the tetrachromacy literature to date.

The latter observation suggests that a bidirectional perceptual consequence associated with the L-180 tetrachromat model may be promising as a potential behavioral marker for identifying tetrachomat phenotypes, especially since the filter approach identifies specific subsets of stimuli that provide the bidirectional predictions that, according to the present findings, permit identification of candidate tetrachromats based purely on color perception variation as assessed by observed color reproduction accuracy.

Finally, the tetrachromat advantage suggested by the Figure 8 results are made more impressive when this countervailing prediction is explicitly considered in analyses. That is, because tetrachromat matching is predicted to be facilitated for some colors and attenuated for others, if we recompute participants' matching errors for only the reddish-and-yellowish set of the "diagnostic" stimuli predicted to capture a tetrachromat perceptual advantage, there is clearly a distinct performance difference between tetrachromat observers compared to normal trichromat observers. This result is presented in Figures 9 and 10.

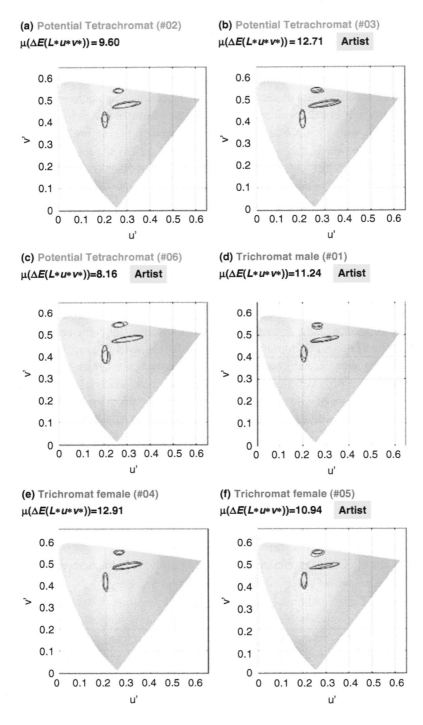

(a) Potential Tetrachromat (#02)

$\mu(\Delta E(L*u*v*)) = 9.60$

(b) Potential Tetrachromat (#03)

$\mu(\Delta E(L*u*v*)) = 12.71$ **Artist**

(c) Potential Tetrachromat (#06)

$\mu(\Delta E(L*u*v*)) = 8.16$ **Artist**

(d) Trichromat male (#01)

$\mu(\Delta E(L*u*v*)) = 11.24$ **Artist**

(e) Trichromat female (#04)

$\mu(\Delta E(L*u*v*)) = 12.91$

(f) Trichromat female (#05)

$\mu(\Delta E(L*u*v*)) = 10.94$ **Artist**

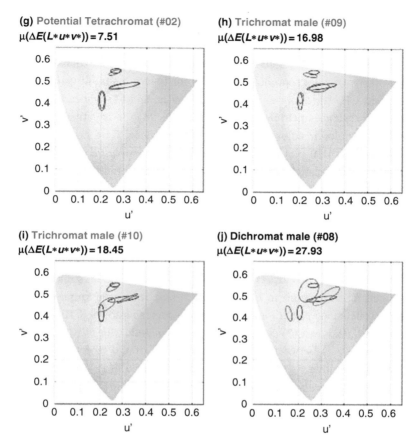

Figure 8 CIELUV color space plots showing Gaussian mixture model solutions for measured reflectances of the 17 Munsell Book of Color stimulus targets in Figure 6 (shown as black ellipses, which are identical across participants) adjacent to contours fit to participant's empirically observed reproductions (shown as blue ellipses, which vary based on participant match performance). Ellipse contours were derived using a Gaussian probability density function to fit groups of colors, with the constraint equal to two standard deviations. In each plot three pairs of ellipses represent solutions fit for three different groupings of target-match-to-sample pairs. That is, ellipses fit to reflectance measures for reddish (six colors), yellowish (five colors), and lavender (six colors) sets, as explained in the results in Section 3 and shown in Figure 6. Plots (a)–(j) depict 10 participants. Potential tetrachromat data are (a)–(c); plots (d)–(i) show trichromats; and plot (j) shows a dichromat. Artist participants are (b), (c), (d), and (f). Each plot presents 17 target stimuli of Figure 6 for one participant's 17 pigment-matches represented in CIELUV space.

3.3.3.5 Examining Average Reproduction Error Differences for Two Subsets of Stimuli

To further clarify the trends seen in Figure 8 we considered interobserver comparisons of color reproduction results for Figure 6 stimuli using both (1) quantified CIE $\Delta E(L*u*v*)$ color differences, and (2) embedded Munsell Euclidean distance metric distances, with the aim of isolating patterns of observer variation in color reproduction performance.

Figures 9 and 10 plot computed *reproduction error difference indices* for individual participants' match performance for the stimuli in Figure 6. The reproduction error difference index is simply the arithmetic difference defined by the average (or mean) measured error for the subset predicted to be *less accurately matched* by an L-180 tetrachromat (i.e., the lavender set) minus the average measured error for the subsets predicted to be *more accurately matched* by an L-180 tetrachromat.

To compute for the CIELUV case we use each participant's match sample produced for the stimuli in Figure 6 to (1) map measured target and match sample reflectance spectra and convert reflectances into the CIELUV space coordinates. We then (2) compute a *match error* index for CIELUV as equal to $\Delta E(L*u*v*)$ between the CIE coordinates of the target stimulus and match color (known as the CIELUV color difference). (3) We next compute a *match error average* over the set of lavender stimuli in Figure 6 ($n = 6$) and the *match error average* for the set of the reddish and yellowish stimuli in Figure 6 ($n = 11$). Finally (4), we define the Reproduction Error Difference Index as the difference between the two *average match error* values computed in (3). Figure 9 depicts these data for the CIELUV color difference computations.

For comparison, Figure 10 depicts analogous computations done for color reproduction measures embedded in a metric Munsell space. This requires only substituting the CIE $\Delta E(L*u*v*)$ values with the corresponding Euclidean distance values computed from reflectance spectra measures embedded in the Munsell Euclidean metric. In general, the pattern of results shown in Figures 9 and 10 are very similar and differ mostly due to a scaling factor variation across the CIE and Munsell Euclidean metrics (scale difference details across histograms are not discussed here).

Two observations can be noted from the results in Figures 9 and 10. First, three potential tetrachromats (participants #02, #03, #06) show Reproduction Error Differences Indices that clearly differentiate them from the pattern found for the group of color vision normal trichromats (participants

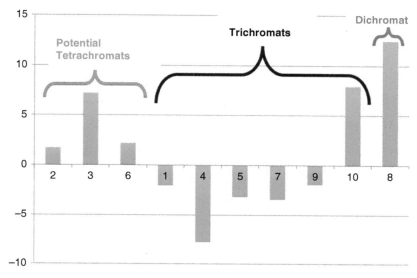

Figure 9 CIE color difference $\Delta E(L*u*v*)$ comparisons of color reproduction performance. Histograms depicting 10 participants' color reproduction data for 17 Munsell stimuli, with individuals grouped by color vision phenotype, identified by participant ID numbers on the abscissa. Each histogram bar plots one participant's color reproduction performance using an index defined as Reproduction error difference index = {[Average match error (lavender stimuli in Figure 6)] minus [Average match error (reddish and yellowish stimuli in Figure 6)]}, where match error is defined according to the color difference index $\Delta E(L*u*v*)$ from CIE $L*u*v*$ color space, where "average" implies an arithmetic mean.

#01, #04, #05, #07, and #09). Also, note that two participants (color vision normal participant #10 and deuteranope participant #08 detailed in the text that follows) are found to essentially fail the task as shown by their abnormally large reproduction errors overall, but the group of five normal trichromats (participants #01, #04, #05, #07, and #09) who, like the tetrachromats assessed, exhibit good color reproduction performance, are found to perform in a manner that differentiates their performance from tetrachromat performance, and, as detailed earlier, do so in a manner predicted by our tetrachromat filter algorithm.

The second point to be noted for the results in Figures 9 and 10 is that depending on the underlying observer model assumed by the metric space used when deriving the Reproduction Error Differences Indices, some potential tetra- chromats may be more accurately modeled than others (see also discussion that follows on various routes to tetrachromacy). This is clearly a topic for further

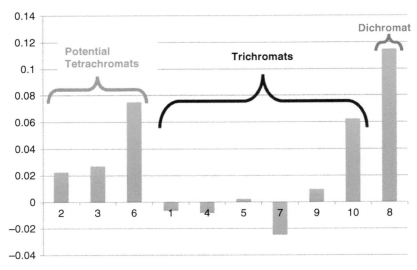

Figure 10 Euclidean distance measure comparisons of color reproduction performance. Histograms depicting 10 participants' color reproduction data for 17 Munsell stimuli, identified by individuals grouped by color vision phenotype, identified by participant ID numbers on the abscissa. Each histogram bar plots one participant's color reproduction performance using an index defined as Reproduction error difference index = {[Average match error (lavender stimuli in Figure 6)] minus [Average match error (reddish and yellowish stimuli in Figure 6)]}, where match error is defined according to the color difference index based on Euclidean distances in a metric Munsell color space, where "average" implies an arithmetic mean.

research because any color appearance space model one might adopt could on the one hand serve adequately for some tetrachromat phenotypes, while alternatively it might be ill-fitted as a model for a different potential tetrachromat's color appearance space, and such a result would impact the appropriateness of interpreting measures of color difference across different tetrachromat phenotypes. In general, if different observer phenotypes require personalized color space metrics in order to compare reproduction match performance in an empirical task, a better, more phenotype-relevant approach to defining an underlying observer model might be needed.

Along these lines, consistent with what has long been established in the literature (e.g., Nagy et al. 1981; Jordan et al. 2010), it is worth noting that, consistent with what has been previously observed, here too not all potential tetrachromats exhibit perceptual variation that differentiates them from trichromats. For example, one of the present study's potential tetrachromats (participant #03, who is also an artist) does not exhibit exceptional measures of color reproduction performance according to the measures in Figures 7 and 8 and is a participant who has previously been described as resembling a "weak tetrachromat" or "retinal tetrachromat" as opposed to a "strong" or "functional" tetrachromat (Bochko and Jameson 2018). Here this participant seems to also be modeled with uncertainty in view of the results in Figures 9 and 10, and is in both cases differentiated from participant #06, who has been extensively studied and who, across a series of investigations, has repeatedly exhibited empirical data distinguishing her from trichromat female controls, indicating a form of functional tetrachromacy (Jameson et al. 2015, 2016, 2018; Atilano et al. 2017, 2020; Bochko et al. 2017; Bochko and Jameson 2018). The tetrachromat variation trends in Figures 9 and 10 are also likely to be influenced by the variable appropriateness of the underlying observer models assumed in their metrics, as well as being impacted by varying levels of tetrachromat processing across potential tetrachromats ranging between "weak" and "strong" extremes (see discussion in Section 4.3). Further research into these subtleties using observer-specific personalized color appearance metrics may help untangle the factors that complicate the utility of the one-size-fits-all standardized metrics provided by existing models of color appearance space.

Finally, it should be noted that the present findings are likely to be specific to the unfiltered D65 illumination experimental condition reported here, which is but one of the three adaptation state conditions that were assessed. Two other adaptation states tested are noted here in the methods for completeness but are planned for reporting elsewhere.

4 Summary and Discussion

In the text that follows we address four issues that deserve consideration in light of the results presented for the empirical study described in Section 3, as well as some relevant issues raised in the review provided in Sections 1 and 2.

4.1 Alternative Routes to Potential Human Tetrachromacy

The present study, much of our previous work, and much of the literature on potential tetrachromacy has focused on investigating perceptual processing in candidate tetrachromats who possess gene sequence dimorphisms at crucial loci that are known to underlie substantial shifts in the spectral separation between, for example, a wild-type L-cone photopigment and a variant L′-cone photopigment (similar to Figure 1b). Our reliance here and elsewhere on the tetrachromat potential of specifically the L-cone-180 serine/alanine heterozygous genotype reflects (1) considerable accumulated knowledge suggesting the L-180 locus is a good, frequently observed, biomarker for potential tetrachromat candidates; and (2) the L-180 locus has a history of successful empirical investigation and modeling for the perceptual correlates of this genotype.

At the same time, we acknowledge that the L-cone-180 heterozygosity that we have studied is but one possible path to potential human tetrachromacy, and that there are a number of other known opsin gene loci in play, as well as other complications presented by gene hybridization and other influential retinal mosaic factors. Some of these include variable optical density of the pigment in the photoreceptors (Shevell et al. 1997; Thomas et al. 2011), highly biased cone ratios (Hofer et al. 2005), and alternative neural processing configurations (cf., "tetrachromacy" of Bongard et al. 1958; Trezona 1973; Brill 1990) that might enhance a path to functional tetrachromacy beyond that provided by the L-180 heterozygous genotype alone. The reality of alternative possible origins for human tetrachromacy further complicates the identification of candidate tetrachromats because it implies that potential color vision tetrachromacy may resemble a probabilistic phenomenon, wherein it is possible to possess multiple kinds of biasing factors that might combine, possibly additively, in ways that would increase the likelihood of experiencing a functioning state of tetrachromat processing. If a candidate tetrachromat were to possess several noteworthy gene sequence alleles – for example, she possessed a heterozygosity for optical density (i.e., SNPs at locus 153) plus heterozygosities at, say, two L-opsin loci (i.e., SNPs at loci 277 and 180) – then clearly adding two or more factors could increase the magnitude or degree of perceptual consequences arising from the expressed tetrachromat phenotype (cf., participant cDA29 from Jordan et al. 2010).

Moreover, tetrachromacy arising from multiple SNPs necessarily increases uncertainty with respect to estimating the frequency of potential tetrachromats arising within a population. Thus, it might be that 47% frequency is expected for potential tetrachromats who are L-180 heterozygotes in the female Caucasian population (Jordan and Mollon 2019), but that additional gene sequence factors contributing to the alternative routes to tetrachromacy might increase this estimated frequency further.

Relevant to the suggested possibility of multiple paths to tetrachromacy, we found a likely case in one of our genotyped female participants (#07) whom we initially considered a trichromat genotype because she is not a carrier for the L-180 heterozygosity. Curiously, however, #07 performed the color reproduction task on a par with our other potential tetrachromat participants. Interestingly, further investigation of #07's genotype subsequently revealed that her excellent color matching performance is likely because she is a potential tetrachromat of an alternative form – namely, she is heterozygous for amino acid dimorphism at OPN1LW-exon 3 at locus 153, by variant substitutions of methionine and leucine. Thus, similar to that described elsewhere (Jordan et al. 2010), our participant #07 possesses an L-153 heterozygosity representing a SNP that should, when alternatively expressed through lyonization, vary the effective optical density of her L-opsin molecule without changing its spectral separation. Changes in optical density have been empirically shown to impact color perception in a manner resembling possession of an additional photopigment class (Shevell et al. 1997; Thomas et al. 2011; Zhaoping and Carroll 2016).

We assume that participant #07 exemplifies an L-cone phenotype that expresses a dimorphic optical density, which is different from the L-180 dimorphic photopigment peak that we tested for, and which can produce a type of potential tetrachromacy with two spectrally distinct L-cone classes being achieved due solely to optical density variation. Systematically detailing the full extent of SNPs and other tetrachromacy factors in play among our participants requires further genotype–phenotype modeling, with the aim being to fully inventory all SNPs that may contribute to the variant forms of potential tetrachromat phenotypes that participants express.

4.2 The Role of Multiple Gene Variants in Color Vision and Potential Tetrachromacy

Uncertainty exists concerning the degree to which multiple gene copies, and different gene variants or hybrids, change the processes that lead to the expression of photopigment classes in the retinal mosaic (Deeb 2005; Neitz and Neitz 2011). Wide ranges of variation can be seen in the expression of the X-linked MWS-to-LWS ratios (i.e., MWS:LWS from 1:1.1 to 1:16.5), and the reasons for this expressed ratio variation remain unclear (Hofer et al. 2005).

More work is also needed to clarify the consequences of different, multiple, gene variants that can occur along the gene array in positions that are far removed from the head of the array where the "locus of control" region interacts with genes and promotes their expression. Several competing hypotheses have appeared in the literature proposing selective expression of LWS versus MWS opsin genes, the latter of which are distal from the locus of the control region on the opsin gene array (Yamaguchi, Motulsky, and Deeb 1997; Shaaban and Deeb 1998; Hayashi, Motulsky, and Deeb 1999). One such hypothesis suggests that, despite the occasional presence of multiple MWS and LWS opsin gene variants in the genetic array, expression mechanisms allow only a single gene variant – that which is most proximal to the locus of control region – to be expressed phenotypically. Thus, in the past the literature has presumed that distal gene variants typically do not become expressed in the retinal phenotype (Sharpe et al. 1998; Winderickx et al. 1992). An alternative viewpoint suggests that multiple LWS opsin genes can be phenotypically expressed (Sjoberg et al. 1998). Moreover, in individuals who have notable heterozygosities in both MWS and LWS opsin genes it might be the case that multiple MWS variants and multiple LWS variants are expressed in the phenotype. Expression of variant forms of both M-cones and L-cones in human retinas is debated, but possession of multiple MWS and LWS opsin gene variants on the head-to-tail opsin gene array may diversify the kinds of tetrachromat phenotypes that are possible (Neitz and Neitz 2011). Research in this area is ongoing and further work on genotype–phenotype relations is needed to clarify the ways retinal mosaics are realized when variant genes for both X–linked opsins are available.

4.3 Age-Related Changes in Color Vision and Potential Tetrachromacy

Research suggests that color perception can change across the lifespan, as wavelength discrimination thresholds increase with age (especially color judgments of the blue-yellow type; Schneck et al. 2014) due to a yellowing of the cornea and lens with age.

Age-related color changes have also recently been shown to interact with the L-180 serine/alanine polymorphism (Dees et al. 2015). The most basic and widespread factors include preretinal filtering effects (e.g., normal age-related lens yellowing) and age-related neural changes (Shinomori et al. 2011).

Consideration of such influences might impact the interpretation of the present empirical results, as two of the three potential tetrachromats (participants #02 and #06) are substantially older (approximately 53.5 years of age) compared to the female trichromat control participants (who on average were approximately 23.6 years of age). This age difference is relevant because it implies that if indeed a tetrachromat phenotype did give rise to subtle advantages in color perception performance as measured by our color reproduction task, then a likely consequence of the age differences of our two participant groups is that it may have the net effect of attenuating the color perception and color processing advantages that are conferred by potential tetrachromacy, thereby decreasing the exceptional color matching performance of a truly functional tetrachromat to a level within the range of normal trichromat matching performance. The implication here is that the impact of potential tetrachromacy reported here might actually be under-estimated due to the age discrepancy across our treatment and control participant groups. Clearly the findings of Dees et al. (2015) for the L-180-serine/alanine polymorphism (which were not known at the time of our study's data collection) highlight the need to secure age-matched control data as a possible oversight in future investigations. However, the present findings remain compelling because the most likely consequence is that the oversight would have diminished or underrepresented the color-matching performance differences observed between our female L-180 heterozygote participants and our female trichromat genotype participants. An important lesson from the Dees et al. work is that seeking out age-matched control data will be an important consideration for future empirical investigations of potential tetrachromacy.

4.4 Color Appearance Space Modeling Under Retinal Tetrachromacy

What color vision modeling impacts are likely to result from the line of research into human potential tetrachromacy? First, let us consider implications for color vision assessment procedures. Because a strictly trivariant model is assumed in nearly all existing diagnostic tools that are traditionally used to identify color anomalous and deficient observers from "normal" trichromats, modifications to these testing methods will be needed to permit detection of color vision varia-tions arising from both weak and strong forms of functional tetrachromacy. In research reviewed earlier, and throughout the work of Jameson and colleagues, this is exemplified in the use of novel, nontraditional, stimulus formats and empirical approaches that employ, comparatively speaking, large-field, binocu-larly viewed, psychophysical and surface color appearance stimuli of the kind that has been largely absent from the study of heterozygous carriers.

Stimulus configurations of the kind described here and in our other work (Jameson et al. 2001, 2006, 2015, 2016, 2018; Sayim et al. 2005; Bochko et al. 2017; Bochko and Jameson 2018) deviate by design from the traditional monocular, small-field, Maxwellian view and anomaloscope-type stimulus formats. Nevertheless, these novel alternatives are exactly what are needed to complement the sharper characterization of photopigments that is now possible through recent innovations in molecular genetic techniques. New, more infor-mative, genetic methods, combined with the use of less impoverished stimuli, provide tools that permit more probative investigations of female opsin gene heterozygotes as compared to female controls who are homozygous for M- and L-opsin genes, in addition to permitting assessment of the impacts of opsin gene hybrids on the expressed phenotypes of males and females.

Research into human tetrachromacy has a potential to overturn conventional wisdom concerning a well-understood system, resulting in a rather basic change in our understanding of color vision, and the expectation is that it should enrich our understanding of empirical measures of the neural trivariance construct (e.g., MacLeod 1985).

A second impact of research on potential tetrachromacy concerns theoretical modeling. We readily admit that the theoretical dichotomy of "weak" versus "strong" forms of functional tetrachromacy is a first-step simplification of the possible continuum of consequences arising from potential tetrachromat genotypes. The literature on the topic characterizes "weak tetrachromacy" as the retinal expression of four distinct photopigment classes in the observer phenotype that nonetheless leads to a normal trichromatic experience. Signals from the four cone types presumably combine – as evidenced by normal trichromat color vision behaviors – to produce a neural color code based on three independent channels (Nagy et al. 1981; Mollon 1989; Jordon and Mollon 1993). "Strong tetrachromacy," by comparison, is also characterized by as the phenotypic expression of four distinct photopigment classes in observers' retinas. However, in the latter case the four cone types give rise to neural signals processed as four independent channels, which can be confirmed by perceptual measures, and which thereby confer an extra functional dimension of perceptual color experience arising from a tetrachromat cortical color code (Mollon 1992; Jordan et al. 2010).

Some researchers have used a statistical modeling approaches to investigate whether color selectivity in the visual system could be the result of a learning process in which, provided sufficient stimulus complexity, more than three cone classes could adaptively form a higher dimensional color code. (e.g., Wachtler et al. 2007). Wachtler et al. conclude, based on an analysis set of 70 natural scenes, that there is insufficient information in natural scenes to support unsupervised learning of signals specific to a fourth cone class. We consider this issue to remain undecided however, and with regard to the view that functional tetrachromacy is computationally untenable, Jordan et al. (2010, p. 15) note " . . . with individual variation in spectral separation, cone ratios, and optical densities, we might expect carriers to display varying degrees of behavioral tetrachromacy, according to the relative amplifications of the normal and the anomalous chromatic signals reaching the cortex. In most cases, the 'anomalous' signal may be masked by a much stronger L/M signal or may be too weak during ontogeny to recruit an independent subset of post-receptoral channels (Wachtler et al. 2007)." Thus the specifics of neural signaling in a empirically observed functional tetrachromat stands as an issue in need of further study.

We caution that a tendency, which can be found in the literature, for a somewhat unsophisticated dichotomous view concerning the consequences of potential trichromacy may be constraining theoretical thinking. Following such a binary line of thinking supposes the polarized perspective that possessing an extra class of retinal photoreceptors either (a) produces no expansion of color vision dimensionality from trichromacy, or (b) creates an additional fully independent color channel which expands color vision dimensionality from the usual three dimensions of trichromacy to four full dimensions of tetrachromacy. Such an all-or-none proposition may be an oversimplification of reality.

Let us consider other plausible alternatives between these extremes. For example, the signal arising from, say, a fourth distinct L'-cone class might actually be only partially correlated with the existing L-cone trichromat signal (because the former duplicates a large portion of the chromatic response of the latter). But then the L'-cone response could also be fully independent for some segment of wavelengths along the chromatic response function profile. Such an arrangement could provide a more narrowly focused signal, one that is independent from the L-cone signal, but only for a specific range of wavelengths. This configuration would have the extra photopigment class contributing to a composite signaling model where independent tetrachromat processing may be manifest in a subarea of color space, but not provide an additional full tetrachromat dimension. Other composite models can be hypothesized, but one example is sufficient to illustrate that the effect of an extra retinal photopigment class might be best modeled along a continuum between the two extremes which characterize tetrachromat color processing influences across the entire color appearance space versus across none of color space.

5 Conclusions

We began with a brief review of the possibility that some individuals might have their color vision supported by four rather than the standard three cone types. Research on this possibility was begun by Nagy et al. (1981) even before it was technically possible to isolate the photopigment opsins by analyzing recombinant DNA. Their work established that the eyes of female carriers of abnormality contained more than three types of cones with different spectral sensitivities. This finding in turn sparked interest in perceptual investigations of X-chromosome-linked factors in female carriers of color vision abnormality, including the question of whether such genetic variation might complicate the dimensional structure of color appearance space.

The central question raised by the work of Nagy et al. (1981) is whether having four degrees of freedom in early retinal signaling fundamentally alters the practical experience of color vision in everyday life and changes the theoretical understanding of color vision through the modeling of signaling from an extra photopiment class. In other words, does a four-dimensional color code – one in which four independent color signals are cortically present – form the basis of some people's color vision. A considerable amount of research has pursued answers to the question posed by the original investigation of Nagy et al. In particular, the 1990s saw significant advances in the study of potential tetrachromats via behavioral research. The subsequent decade saw further advances through the adoption of methods to study surface color appearances (Bimler et al. 2004; Bosten et al. 2005; Sayim et al. 2005; Jordan et al. 2010). The present study, along with others we have reviewed, converges on the conclusion that for some small areas of the color appearance space, functional, or "strong," human tetrachromacy is a phenomenologically real and empirically measurable experience.

Future progress on this topic will depend on the development of novel ways for empirically investigating how to assess, model, and analyze potential tetrachromacy. It is now important to clarify differences across the entire color appearance space that may exist for tetrachromats, and to clarify how those compare beyond the individual variations already seen among trichromat observers. Our work in this area is only now beginning to answer the questions concerning potential tetrachromacy that Nagy et al. (1981) originally raised.

This Element has described new approaches for quantifying tetrachromat performance differences, adding to those that were indicated in previous work using nonnegative matrix factorization (NMF) machine learning approaches (Bochko and Jameson 2018).

The new empirical data we reported showed that eight of nine participants with "normal" color vision excelled in a novel color reproduction task. Their color matching data in conjunction with full opsin genotyping (Atilano et al. 2020) helped to identify and characterize alternative forms of color vision. The ways in which the perceptual experience of these participants deviated from the ranges known for normal color vision trichromacy correlated in systematic ways with their identifiable opsin gene markers.

These data are presented as a proof of concept that the novel approach presented here can help clarify the perceptual impacts that are possible through potential tetrachromat processing involving specific L-cone gene variants. They also bolster earlier results and theory presented by Jameson et al. (2015, 2016) and Bochko and Jameson (2018) suggesting that potential tetrachromats may not always deviate from a standard trichromat model. Moreover, when they do deviate from standard trichromacy, it may be in ways that do not impact perception across the whole of color appearance space. Indeed, tetrachromat color processing variation may not require the standard trichromat model to newly accommodate a full tetrachromat dimension, but rather may be more in line with MacLeod and von der Twer's "split range" neural code type models (MacLeod and von der Twer 2003) involving a rectified half dimension as the basis of color vision processing variation conferred by tetrachromat retinas.

Appendix

(1) Illuminant properties.

Three experiments conducted differed only by virtue of using three different illumination conditions. One illumination condition was an unfiltered D65 approximation shown in Figure A1. Two other illumination conditions (assessed after the D65 illumination condition and not reported here) consisted of filtering the Figure A1 illuminant with a chromatic filter or a neutral density achromatic filter. (The other two illuminant spectral power distributions are not shown).

(2) Evaluating pigment palette adequacy for the reproduction task.

Before analyzing participants' color matching performance we first sought to investigate the adequacy of the uniform pigment set used in the experiments, for the purpose of determining the appropriateness of the palette to reproduce the 41 target colors assessed. Ideally in our reproduction task the palette employed should easily allow pigment mixture combinations that satisfy an exact or very close match to a target color. These pigment analyses aimed to determine the palette's appropriateness for reproducing the color stimuli we tested. For the purposes of comparing the correspondence between the measured reflectance spectra of target stimuli and matched samples we first needed to assess the differences observed in reflectance spectra measures when pigments were wet (as they were when used by participants performing matching judgments on the reproduction task) compared to when pigments were fully dry (as when spectroradiometric measures were made several days after participants created matched samples through the reproduction task). Our analyses (shown earlier in Figure 4) found that wet and dry oil pigments used in the experimental palette were nearly identical, as measured by ΔE values, derived using the CIEDE2000 color-difference formula.

Next our initial analyses sought to algorithmically evaluate all of the palette's pigment reflectance spectra and identify the pigment mixtures that could potentially achieve replication of target reflectance spectra. Most existing paint mixing algorithms require advance knowledge of the specific amounts of paints used in the match mix (Berns 2004). This is not the case here; we only know the spectra of the targets and the spectra of the palette paints. We don't know which paints were used in a given participant's mix. Moreover, two different spectral distributions can be metamers of one another, which makes minimizing the error between spectra problematic. Thus, our initial algorithmic evaluation of pigment mixtures was indeterminant.

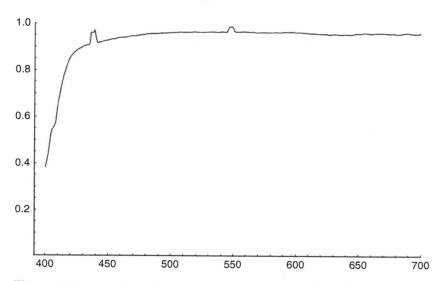

Figure A1 Measured spectral power distribution of D65 illuminant used in all experiments. Spikes seen in the otherwise smooth illuminant spectrum are a property of the D65 fluorescent lamp's spectral power distribution.

For these reasons we abandoned the algorithmic evaluation of the palette mixtures and instead chose to identify the minimum empirically observed error found between painted target reproductions and their source targets. The rationale was that if participants were able to employ the palette to successfully produce good approximations of target color reflectances, then this was an indication that the palette was adequate for the reproduction task for the stimulus set tested.

To evaluate the minimum observed match error we used Euclidean distances between Munsell embedded targets and painted samples and quantified the smallest and the largest observed match errors. We reasoned that minimum errors indicated whether the palette was sufficient for participants to produce a color appearance that closely matched the target appearance in Munsell space. For such cases minimum error would thus represent the best observed match empirically achieved between a sample and a target, and thereby demonstrated the palette's appropriateness for the task and for our participants.

Thus, we evaluated the minimum Euclidean distance in Munsell space across all subjects for each target–reproduction pair, because this value represents the best match between target and sample for any subject. The reason we consider this the maximum amount of error attributable to the palette for paint mixtures between target and sample is that (1) all subjects used the same palette paints, (2) we can infer for the participant with the smallest reproduction error that at least one of the subjects we tested was attempting to accomplish the target–sample match as best as he or she

Munsell Chips (Value 5) & 41 Targets
with Maximum Palette Error

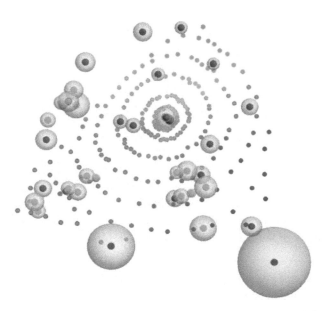

Figure A2 Evaluating the adequacy of the standardized paint palette (Figure 4) that participants were provided for the task of reproducing target color stimuli. For each of the 41 target stimuli all participant's palette pigment reflectance measurements were analyzed to identify the best-fitting match to the target that was empirically achieved. The plot shows 41 stimuli with their computed best-fitting mixtures as bubble contours. Image depicts coronal plane view of the Munsell color space, looking directly down the Munsell Value axis, onto the top of the Value = 5 plane. The 24 Macbeth ColorChecker stimulus targets are shown as black dots and 17 Munsell color stimulus targets as red dots. Each of the 41 target stimuli is centered in a bubble depicting the computed Euclidean distance minimum that was empirically realized as a match for each target stimulus. Thus, minimal contours for each target indicate the best observed reproduction of the target that was achieved in our experiments by at least one participant's painted match, given the same standard pigment palette all participants used.

could, and (3) there is no guarantee that the subjects used the optimal set of palette paints in the correct proportions. However, if they did then the palette paint mixture they used is the best possible. If not, there are other mixtures of palette paints and their proportions that could possibly be better. Given this rationale we assume the

**Munsell Chips (Value 5) & 41 Targets
with Maximum Palette Error**

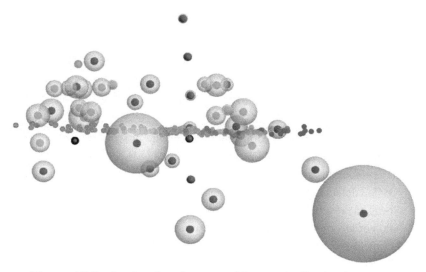

Figure A3 Evaluating the adequacy of the standardized paint palette (Figure 4) that participants were provided for the task of reproducing target color stimuli. Same computation and caption as in Figure A2, although here the image shown is a sagittal view of the Munsell color space, looking edge-on at Value = 5 plane.

minimum Euclidean distance across all subjects for any target–sample pair to be the maximum error that can be imparted by the choice of palette primaries for this task.

The result of this analysis is represented in Figures A2 and A3. These figures show, for each of the 41 target stimuli and an associated sphere, where the size of the sphere conveys the relative size of the observed Euclidean distance minima, which indicates the best degree of fit realizable between the target sample and its reproduction with the standard pigment palette used. Spheres shown are centered on the target color in Munsell space and sphere radii are made equal to the minimum Euclidean distance for the best observed reproduction across all study participants.

Glossary

Adapting annulus   A colored surround (usually a circular disk, or "annulus") in which a central test field is centered for adjustment and judgment. The surrounding annulus provides a minimal relational stimulus structure that is sufficient for formal modeling (see Mausfeld and Niederée 1993) and is the standard psychophysical way of providing a viewing context that allows for adaptation type effects that approximate a naturalistic viewing mode (Nagy et al. 1981; Jordan and Mollon 1993).

Anomaloscope   Optical instruments in which the observer must manipulate stimulus control knobs to match two colored fields in color and brightness. The anomaloscope is the standard instrument for the diagnosis of color vision defects. When supplemented by information from other color vision tests, the results provided by this instrument permit the accurate classification of all color deficiencies. It is agreed that the anomaloscope is the only clinical method capable of classifying color defects by their presumed genetic entities. However, it was designed only to detect color deficiencies, and not designed to detect tetrachromacy-based deviations from normal color vision.

Chromaphore   The chromophore exists in a pocket of the opsin molecule that serves to capture or detect light energy and is the cause of conformational change of the molecule, and the initiation of the phototransduction process, when hit by photons of light.

Chromatic response functions   The response sensitivity curves that peak at points in the visible spectrum where a particular photoreceptor class responds and are at the basis of formal color vision models.

Dimorphic   Meaning "of two forms," as in "dimorphic optical density" which is when a given cone class has two kinds of cells that are otherwise identical except for the density of the optical pigment within the different forms. Or "dimorphic photopigment peak," when a given class of photoreceptors has two sets of cell classes expressed that respond with distinctly different peak response profiles (as in the L-180-serine-alanine heterozygote).

Farnsworth–Munsell 100 Hue test   The Farnsworth–Munsell 100 Hue Color Vision test is a standardized test for color blindness. It was developed in the 1940s and is still widely used today. It tests the ability to isolate and arrange minute differences in various color targets by sorting colors into a smooth gradient of hue at constant saturation.

Ishihara Pseudo-isochromatic Plates   A book of plates that consists of sets of colored dotted plates, each of them showing either a number or a path. Detection of the numbers or paths is apparent only if the test taker is not color deficient. Performance on particular plates determines the form of an observer's deficiency. It is a very widely used color vision deficiency test and still used by most optometrists and ophthalmologists all around the world.

Locus of control region   The genetic sequence region at the head of the opsin gene array that dictates which genes within a sequential line on the array get expressed.

M- and L-opsin genes   X-chromosome-linked genes that respond maximally at medium (M-) and long (L-) wavelengths of the visible spectrum. Also abbreviated as MWS for "medium-wavelength sensitive" and LWS for "long-wavelength sensitive," respectively.

Maxwellian view   Stimuli when viewed with one eye through a viewing lens similar to a telescopic eyepiece. The color appearance of lights that pass through a small portion of the center of the natural pupil (Maxwellian view) is not the same as when the same lights, at the same retinal illuminance, pass through all parts of the natural pupil (Newtonian view). See Gordon and Abramov (2008).

Nonnegative matrix factorization (NMF) machine learning approaches   Nonnegative matrix factorization (NMF) is a common machine learning approach that provides useful nonnegative decompositions used here to analyze color matching spectral reflectance measure data. NMF can define optimal nonnegative representations of spectral colors for data from different sets of stimuli (see Bochko and Jameson 2018).

Opsin gene heterozygotes   Individuals with different allelic variants of a given (M- or L-opsin) photopigment opsin gene on each of two X chromosomes.

Opsin genes   Genetic sequences with different amino acid sequences and a light-absorbing chromaphore can produce photoreceptor classes with drastically different responses to visible light.

Rayleigh matching procedure   A technique for matching a particular yellow appearance with a red plus green mixture while viewing the stimulus in an otherwise dark environment with one eye through an eyepiece. Lord Rayleigh (1881) invented a color mixing apparatus that employed narrow spectral bands of red and green to match yellow, discovered that a few observers made matches that were very different from those made by the majority of other observers.

Rectified half dimensions   A concept in the modeling of neural signaling, also called a "split range code," used by the visual system. The concept posits that separate neurons respond to inputs on opposite sides of that null point rather than the usual idea of responding along the continuous range of a dimension. According to MacLeod and von der Twer (2003): By adopting a split range code, and representing opposite segments of the input range by neurons that each have rectifying and compressive response nonlinearities, the visual system maximizes the average precision in its representation of natural inputs in the presence of neural noise introduced at the output.

Rods and cones   Retina receptor classes that transmit visual signal from the eye to the brain. Rod cells are maximally sensitive in low light conditions, or scotopic light levels. Cones respond primarily in bright light, or photopic levels, and are responsible for color vision.

Single-nucleotide polymorphism (SNP)   A single nucleotide change, or variant, in the opsin gene sequence is called a single nucleotide polymorphism or SNP. A SNP can cause a change in the amino acid of an opsin protein, which in turn can produce a dramatic shift in the visual response to light.

Tetrachromacy   In its minimal sense, refers to the possession of four rather than three types of cone photoreceptor cell classes in the retina of the eyes.

References

Asenjo, A. B., Rim, J., and Oprian, D. D. (1994). Molecular determinants of human red/green color discrimination. *Neuron, 12*(5), 1131–1138.

Atilano, S., Jameson, K. A., and Kenney, M. C. (2017). Procedures for characterizing the genetic sequences underlying human visual phenotypes: Genotyping methods and a case-study demonstration. *Technical Report Series # MBS 17–05.* Institute for Mathematical Behavioral Sciences, University of California at Irvine. Available at www.imbs.uci.edu/research/MBS%2017–05.pdf

Shari, R. Atilano, M. Cristina Kenney, Adriana D. Briscoe, and Kimberly A. Jameson. (2020). "A two-step method for identifying photopigment opsin and rhodopsin gene sequences underlying human color vision phenotypes." Molecular Vision; 26:158–172 <http://www.molvis.org/molvis/v26/158>

Balding, S. D., Sjoberg, S. A., Neitz, J., and Neitz, M. (1998). Pigment gene expression in protan color vision defects. *Vision Research, 38*(21), 3359–3364.

Berns, R. S. (2004). Rejuvenating Seurat's palette using color and imaging science: A simulation. In R. L. Herbert (ed.), *Seurat and the making of La Grande Jatte*, 214–227. The Art Institute of Chicago and University of California Press.

Bimler, D., and Kirkland, J. (2009). Colour-space distortion in women who are heterozygous for colour deficiency. *Vision Research, 49*(5), 536–543.

Bimler, D. L., Kirkland, J., and Jameson, K. A. (2004). Quantifying variations in personal color spaces: Are there sex differences in color vision? *COLOR Research and Application, 29*(2), 128–134.

Birch, J. (2001). *Diagnosis of defective colour vision*, 24–29. Oxford: Butterworth-Heinemann.

Bochko, V. A., and Jameson, K. A. (2018). Investigating potential human tetrachromacy in individuals with tetrachromat genotypes using multispectral techniques. *Electronic Imaging*, 2018(14), 1–12.

Bochko, V. A., Jameson, K. A., Nakaguchi T., Miyake Y., and Alander J. T. (2017). Non-negative matrix factorization for spectral colors using genetic algorithms: Substantially Updated Version. *IMBS Technical Report Series #MBS 17–03.* Institute for Mathematical Behavioral Sciences University of California at Irvine, Irvine, CA. Available at www.imbs.uci.edu/research/MBS%2017–03.pdf

Bongard, M. M., Smirnov, M. S., and Friedrich, L. I. (1958). The four-dimensional colour space of the extra-foveal retinal area of the human eye. In *Visual problems of colour I*, 325–330. London: HMSO.

Bosten, J. M., Robinson, J. D., Jordan, G., and Mollon, J. D. (2005). Multidimensional scaling reveals a color dimension unique to 'color-deficient' observers. *Current Biology, 15*(23), R950–R952.

Bowmaker, J. K., Astell, S., Hunt, D. M., and Mollon, J. D. (1991). Photosensitive and photostable pigments in the retinae of Old World monkeys. *Journal of Experimental Biology, 156*(1), 1–19.

Bowmaker, J. K., and Dartnall, H. (1980). Visual pigments of rods and cones in a human retina. *The Journal of Physiology, 298*(1), 501–511.

Bowmaker, J. K., Dartnall, H. J., Lythgoe, J. N., and Mollon, J. D. (1978). The visual pigments of rods and cones in the rhesus monkey, *Macaca mulatta. Journal of Physiology, 274*(1), 329–348.

Brill, M. H. (1990). Mesopic color matching: Some theoretical issues. *Journal of the Optical Society of America A, 7*(10), 2048–2051.

Carroll, J., Gray, D. C., Roorda, A., and Williams, D. R. (2005). Recent advances in retinal imaging with Percher optics. *Optics and Photonics News, 16*(1), 36–42.

Changizi, M. A., Zhang, Q., and Shimojo, S. (2006). Bare skin, blood and the evolution of primate colour vision. *Biology Letters, 2*(2), 217–221.

Crognale, M. A., Teller, D. Y., Motulsky, A. G., and Deeb, S. S. (1998). Severity of color vision defects: Electroretinographic (ERG), molecular and behavioral studies. *Vision Research, 38*(21), 3377–3385.

Dalton, J. (1798). *Extraordinary facts relating to the vision of colours: With observations.* London: Cadell and Davies.

Dartnall, H. J., Bowmaker, J. K., and Mollon, J. D. (1983). Human visual pigments: Microspectrophotometric results from the eyes of seven persons. *Proceedings of the Royal Society of London B: Biological Sciences, 220* (1218), 115–130.

Deeb, S. S. (2004). Molecular genetics of color-vision deficiencies. *Visual Neuroscience, 21*(3), 191–196.

Deeb, S. S. (2005). The molecular basis of variation in human color vision. *Clinical Genetics, 67*(5), 369–377.

Dees, E. W., and Baraas, R. C. (2014). Performance of normal females and carriers of color-vision deficiencies on standard color-vision tests. *Journal of the Optical Society of America A, 31*(4), A401–A409.

Dees, E. W., Gilson, S. J., Neitz, M., and Baraas, R. C. (2015). The influence of L-opsin gene polymorphisms and neural ageing on spatio-chromatic contrast sensitivity in 20–71 year olds. *Vision Research, 116*, 13–24.

Dominy, N. J., and Lucas, P. W. (2001). Ecological importance of trichromatic vision to primates. *Nature, 410*(6826), 363.

Farnsworth, D. (1949, revised 1957). *The Farnsworth-Munsell 100-Hue test for the examination of color vision.* Baltimore, MD: Munsell Color Company.

Feil, R., Aubourg, P., Heilig, R., and Mandel, J. L. (1990). A 195-kb cosmid walk encompassing the human Xq28 color vision pigment genes. *Genomics, 6*(2), 367–373.

Fernandez, A. A., and Morris, M. R. (2007). Sexual selection and trichromatic color vision in primates: Statistical support for the preexisting-bias hypothesis. *American Naturalist, 170*(1), 10–20.

Gardner, J. C., Liew, G., Quan, Y. H., et al. (2014). Three different cone opsin gene array mutational mechanisms with genotype–phenotype correlation and functional investigation of cone opsin variants. *Human Mutation, 35*(11), 1354–1362. DOI:10.1002/humu.22679.

Gegenfurtner, K. R., and Sharpe, L. T. (eds.). (1999). Color vision: From genes to perception. Cambridge: Cambridge University Press.

Gordon, J., and Abramov, I. (2008). Color appearance: Maxwellian vs. Newtonian views. *Vision Research, 48*(18), 1879–1883.

Hagstrom, S. A., Neitz, J., and Neitz, M. (1998). Variations in cone populations for red–green color vision examined by analysis of mRNA. *NeuroReport, 9*(9), 1963–1967.

Hayashi, T., Motulsky, A. G., and Deeb, S. S. (1999). Position of a 'green-red 'hybrid gene in the visual pigment array determines colour-vision phenotype. *Nature Genetics, 22*(1), 90.

He, J. C., and Shevell, S. K. (1995). Variation in color matching and discrimination among deuteranomalous trichromats: Theoretical implications of small differences in photopigments. *Vision Research, 35*(18), 2579–2588.

Hofer, H., Carroll, J., Neitz, J., Neitz, M., and Williams, D. R. (2005). Organization of the human trichromatic cone mosaic. *Journal of Neuroscience, 25*(42), 9669–9679.

Hood, S. M., Mollon, J. D., Purves, L., and Jordan, G. (2006). Color discrimination in carriers of color deficiency. *Vision Research, 46*(18), 2894-2900.

Ishihara, S. (1989). *Ishihara's tests for colour blindness: Concise 14 plate edition.* Tokyo: Kanehara.

Jacobs, G. H. (1998). Photopigments and seeing: Lessons from natural experiments: The Proctor lecture. *Investigative Ophthalmology and Visual Science, 39*(12), 2204.

Jacobs, G. H. (2008). Primate color vision: A comparative perspective. *Visual Neuroscience, 25*(5–6), 619–633.

Jacobs, G. H. (2018). Photopigments and the dimensionality of animal color vision. *Neuroscience and Biobehavioral Reviews, 86*, 108–130.

Jacobs, G. H., and Nathans, J. (2009). The evolution of primate color vision. *Scientific American, 300*(4), 56–63.

Jameson, K. A. (2009). Tetrachromatic color vision. In *The Oxford companion to consciousness,* 155–158. Oxford: Oxford University Press.

Jameson K. A., Bimler D., and Wasserman L. M. (2006). Re–assessing perceptual diagnostics for observers with diverse retinal photopigment genotypes. In N. J. Pitchford and C. P. Biggam, eds.), *Progress in colour studies,* Vol. 2: *Cognition,* 13–33. Amsterdam: John Benjamins.

Jameson K. A., Bochko V. A., Joe K. C., Satalich T. A., and Atilano S. R. (2018). Color processing in artists and non-artist participants in relation to individually determined photopigment opsin genotypes. In *Munsell Centennial Color Symposium: Bridging science, art, & industry,* June 10–15, 2018, Massachusetts College of Art and Design, Boston.

Jameson, K. A., Highnote, S. M., and Wasserman, L. M. (2001). Richer color experience in observers with multiple photopigment opsin genes. *Psychonomic Bulletin & Review, 8*(2), 244–261.

Jameson, K. A., Wasserman, L., and Highnote, S. (1998a). Photopigment opsin genes and color perception. Poster presented at the Annual Meeting of the Optical Society of America, October 1–4, 1998, Baltimore, MD.

Jameson, K. A., Wasserman, L., and Highnote, S. (1998b). Understanding color appearance: Can variation in photopigment opsin genes give rise to individuals with perceptual tetrachromacy? Poster presented at the 21st European Conference of Visual Perception, August 24–28, 1998, Oxford.

Jameson, K. A., Winkler, A. D., and Goldfarb, K. (2016). Art, interpersonal comparisons of color experience, and potential tetrachromacy. *Electronic Imaging,* 2016(16), 1–12.

Jameson, K. A., Winkler, A. D., Herrera, C., and Goldfarb, K. (2014). The veridicality of color: A case study of potential human tetrachromacy. Technical Report Series# MBS 14-02. Institute for Mathematical Behavioral Sciences University of California at Irvine. Irvine, CA. www.imbs.uci.edu/files/imbs/docs/technical/2014/mbs 14-02. pdf

Jameson, K. A. (2009). Tetrachromatic color vision. In *The Oxford companion to consciousness* (pp. 155–158). Oxford Press Oxford.

Jordan, G., Deeb, S. S., Bosten, J. M., and Mollon, J. D. (2010). The dimensionality of color vision in carriers of anomalous trichromacy. *Journal of Vision, 10*(8), 1–19 DOI:10.1167/10.8.12.

Jordan, G., and Mollon, J. D. (1993). A study of women heterozygous for colour deficiencies. *Vision Research, 33*(11), 1495–1508.

Jordan, G., and Mollon, J. (2019). Tetrachromacy: The mysterious case of extra-ordinary color vision. *Current Opinion in Behavioral Sciences*, *30*, 130–134.

Konstantakopoulou, E., Rodriguez-Carmona, M., and Barbur, J. L. (2012). Processing of color signals in female carriers of color vision deficiency. *Journal of Vision*, *12*(2), 1–11. DOI:10.1167/12.2.11.

Liebman, P. A. (1972). Microspectrophotometry of photoreceptors. In *Photochemistry of vision*, 481–528. Berlin, Heidelberg: Springer-Verlag.

Lucas, P. W., Dominy, N. J., Riba-Hernandez, P., et al. (2003). Evolution and function of routine trichromatic vision in primates. *Evolution*, *57*(11), 2636–2643.

Luo, M. R., Cui, G., and Rigg, B. (2001). The development of the CIE 2000 colour-difference formula: CIEDE2000. *COLOR Research and Application*, *26*(5), 340–350.

Macbeth (2014). ColorChecker Classic. X-Rite Pantone, Grand Rapids, MI.

MacLeod, D. I. A. (1985). Receptoral constraints on colour appearance. In *Central and peripheral mechanisms of colour vision*, 103–116. London: Palgrave Macmillan.

MacLeod, D. I. A., and von der Twer, T. (2003). The pleistochrome: Optimal opponent codes for natural colours. *Colour Perception: Mind and the Physical World*, 155–184.

Mausfeld, R., and Niederée, R. (1993). An inquiry into relational concepts of colour, based on incremental principles of colour coding for minimal relational stimuli. *Perception*, *22*(4), 427–462.

Merbs, S. L., and Nathans, J. (1992a). Absorption spectra of human cone pigments. *Nature*, *356*(6368), 433.

Merbs, S. L., and Nathans, J. (1992b). Absorption spectra of the hybrid pigments responsible for anomalous color vision. *Science*, *258*(5081), 464–466.

Merbs, S. L., and Nathans, J. (1993). Role of hydroxyl-bearing amino acids in differentially tuning the absorption spectra of the human red and green cone pigments. *Photochemistry and Photobiology*, *58*(5), 706–710.

Mollon, J. (1992). Worlds of difference. *Nature*, *356*, 2.

Mollon, J. D. (1989). "Tho'she kneel'd in that place where they grew ... " The uses and origins of primate colour vision. *Journal of Experimental Biology*, *146*(1), 21–38.

Moore, C., Romney, A. K., and Hsia, T. L. (2002). Cultural, gender, and individual differences in perceptual and semantic structures of basic colors in Chinese and English. *Journal of Cognition and Culture*, *2*(1), 1–28.

Munsell (1976). Munsell book of color: Matte finish collection. Munsell Color, Inc., Baltimore, MD.

Nagy, A. L., MacLeod, D. I., Heyneman, N. E., and Eisner, A. (1981). Four cone pigments in women heterozygous for color deficiency. *Journal of the Optical Society of America*, *71*(6), 719–722.

Nathans, J., Merbs, S. L., Sung, C. H., Weitz, C. J., and Wang, Y. (1992). Molecular genetics of human visual pigments. *Annual Review of Genetics*, *26* (1), 403–424.

Nathans, J., Piantanida, T. P., Eddy, R. L., Shows, T. B., and Hogness, D. S. (1986a). Molecular genetics of inherited variation in human color vision. *Science*, *232*(4747), 203–210.

Nathans, J., Thomas, D., and Hogness, D. S. (1986b). Molecular genetics of human color vision: The genes encoding blue, green, and red pigments. *Science*, *232*(4747), 193–202.

Neitz, J., and Jacobs, G. H. (1986). Polymorphism of the long-wavelength cone in normal human colour vision. *Nature*, *323*(6089), 623–625.

Neitz, J., and Jacobs, G. H. (1990). Polymorphism in normal human color vision and its mechanism. *Vision Research*, *30*(4), 621–636.

Neitz, J., and Neitz, M. (2011). The genetics of normal and defective color vision. *Vision Research*, *51*(7), 633–651. DOI:10.1016/j.visres.2010.12.002. Epub 2010 Dec 15. Review.

Neitz, M., and Neitz, J. (1998). Molecular genetics and the biological basis of color vision. *Color Vision: Perspectives from Different Disciplines*, *101*, 119.

Neitz, M., Neitz, J., and Grishok, A. (1995). Polymorphism in the number of genes encoding long-wavelength sensitive cone pigments among males with normal colour vision. *Vision Research*, *35*, 2395–2407.

Neitz, M., Neitz, J., and Jacobs, G. H. (1991). Spectral tuning of pigments underlying red-green color vision. *Science*, *252*(5008), 971–974.

Neitz, J., Neitz, M., and Jacobs, G. H. (1993). More than three different cone pigments among people with normal color vision. *Vision Research*, *33*(1), 117–122.

Neitz, M., Neitz, J., and Jacobs, G. H. (1995). Genetic basis of photopigment variations in human dichromats. *Vision Research*, *35*(15), 2095–2103.

Osorio, D., and Vorobyev, M. (1996). Colour vision as an adaptation to frugivory in primates. *Proceedings of the Royal Society of London B: Biological Sciences*, *263*(1370), 593–599.

Pircher, M., and Zawadzki, R. (2017). Review of adaptive optics OCT (AO-OCT): Principles and applications for retinal imaging. *Biomedical Optics Express*, 8, 2536–2562.

Regan, B. C., Julliot, C., Simmen, B., Viénot, F., Charles–Dominique, P., and Mollon, J. D. (2001). Fruits, foliage and the evolution of primate colour vision. *Philosophical Transactions of the Royal Society of London B: Biological Sciences, 356*(1407), 229–283.

Sanocki, E., Lindsey, D. T., Winderickx, J., Teller, D. Y., Deeb, S. S., and Motulsky, A. G. (1993). Serine/alanine amino acid polymorphism of the L and M cone pigments: Effects on Rayleigh matches among deuteranopes, protanopes and color normal observers. *Vision Research, 33*(15), 2139–2152.

Sanocki, E., Shevell, S. K., and Winderickx, J. (1994). Serine/alanine amino acid polymorphism of the L-cone photopigment assessed by dual Rayleigh-type color matches. *Vision Research, 34*(3), 377–382.

Satalich, T. (2015). Modeling color appearance. Paper presented at IMBS Conference, November 5–6, 2015, University of California, Irvine.

Sayim, B., Jameson, K. A., Alvarado, N., and Szeszel, M. (2005). Semantic and perceptual representations of color: Evidence of a shared color-naming function. *Journal of Cognition and Culture, 5*(3–4), 427–486.

Schanda, J. (2007). CIE colorimetry. In *Colorimetry: Understanding the CIE system*, 37–46. Hoboken, NJ: John Wiley & Sons.

Schnapf, J. L., Kraft, T. W., and Baylor, D. A. (1987). Spectral sensitivity of human cone photoreceptors. *Nature, 325*(6103), 439.

Schnapf, J. L., Kraft, T. W., Nunn, B. J., and Baylor, D. A. (1988). Spectral sensitivity of primate photoreceptors. *Visual Neuroscience, 1*(3), 255–261.

Schneck, M. E., Haegerstrom-Portnoy, G., Lott, L. A., and Brabyn, J. A. (2014). Comparison of panel D-15 tests in a large Older Population. *Optometry and Vision Science, 91*(3): 284–290. DOI:10.1097/OPX.0000000000000152.

Shaaban, S. A., and Deeb, S. S. (1998). Functional analysis of the promoters of the human red and green visual pigment genes. *Investigative Ophthalmology & Visual Science, 39*(6), 885–896.

Sharpe, L. T., Stockman, A., Jägle, H., Knau, H., Klausen, G., Reitner, A., and Nathans, J. (1998). Red, green, and red-green hybrid pigments in the human retina: correlations between deduced protein sequences and psychophysically measured spectral sensitivities. *Journal of Neuroscience, 18*(23), 10053–10069.

Shepard, R. N., and Cooper, L. A. (1992). Representation of colors in the blind, color-blind, and normally sighted. *Psychological Science, 3*(2), 97–104.

Shevell, S. K., and He, J. C. (1997). The visual photopigments of simple deuteranomalous trichromats inferred from color matching. *Vision Research, 37*(9), 1115–1127.

Shevell, S. K., He, J. C., Kainz, P., Neitz, J., and Neitz, M. (1998). Relating color discrimination to photopigment genes in deutan observers. *Vision Research, 38*(21), 3371–3376.

Shinomori, K., Schefrin, B. E., and Werner, J. S. (2001). Age-related changes in wavelength discrimination. *Journal of the Optical Society of America A, 18* (2), 310–318.

Shyue, S. K., Boissinot, S., Schneider, H., et al. (1998). Molecular genetics of spectral tuning in New World monkey color vision. *Journal of Molecular Evolution, 46*(6), 697–702.

Sjoberg, S. A., Neitz, M., Balding, S. D., and Neitz, J. (1998). L-cone pigment genes expressed in normal colour vision. *Vision Research, 38*(21), 3213–3219.

Smith, T., and Guild, J. (1931). The CIE colorimetric standards and their use. *Transactions of the Optical Society, 33*(3), 73.

Smith, V.C. and Pokorny, J. (1975). Spectral sensitivity of the foveal cone photopigments between 400 and 500 nm. Vision Research; *15*(2): 161–171. DOI:10.1016/0042–6989(75)90203–5

Sparkes, R. S., Klisak, I., Kaufman, D., Mohandas, T., Tobin, A. J., and McGinnis, J. F. (1986). Assignment of the rhodopsin gene to human chromosome three, region 3q21–3q24 by in situ hybridization studies. *Current Eye Research, 5*(10), 797–798.

Stockman, A. and Sharpe, L.T. (2000). The spectral sensitivities of the middle- and long-wavelength- sensitive cones derived from measurements in observers of known genotype. Vision Research; *40*(13): 1711–1737. DOI:10.1016/S0042–6989(00)00021–3

Sumner, P., and Mollon, J. D. (2003). Colors of primate pelage and skin: Objective assessment of conspicuousness. *American Journal of Primatology, 59*(2), 67–91.

Sun, Y., and Shevell, S. K. (2008). Rayleigh matches in carriers of inherited color vision defects: The contribution from the third L/M photopigment. *Visual Neuroscience, 25*(3), 455–462.

Thomas, P. B. M., Formankiewicz, M. A., and Mollon, J. D. (2011). The effect of photopigment optical density on the color vision of the anomalous trichromat. *Vision Research, 51*(20), 2224–2233.

Trezona, P. W. (1973). The tetrachromatic colour match as a colorimetric technique. *Vision Research, 13*(1), 9–25.

Vollrath, D., Nathans, J., and Davis, R. W. (1988). Tandem array of human visual pigment genes at Xq28. *Science, 240*(4859), 1669–1672.

Wachtler, T., Doi, E., Lee, T.-W., and Sejnowski, T. J. (2007). Cone selectivity derived from the responses of the retinal cone mosaic to natural scenes. *Journal of Vision, 7*(8), 6,1–14. Available at www.journalofvision.org/content/7/8/6, DOI:10.1167/7.8.6.

Wang, Y., Smallwood, P. M., Cowan, M., Blesh, D., Lawler, A., and Nathans, J. (1999). Mutually exclusive expression of human red and green visual pigment-reporter transgenes occurs at high frequency in murine cone photoreceptors. *Proceedings of the National Academy of Sciences of the USA*, *96*(9), 5251–5256.

Wasserman, L. M., Szeszel, M. K., and Jameson, K. A. (2009). Long-range polymerase chain reaction analysis for specifying photopigment opsin gene polymorphisms. *Technical Report Series# MBS 09–07*. Institute for Mathematical Behavioral Sciences University of California at Irvine, Irvine, CA. Available at www.imbs.uci.edu/files/docs/technical/2009/mbs_ 09–07.pdf

Winderickx, J., Lindsey, D. T., Sanocki, E., Teller, D. Y., Motulsky, A. G., and Deeb, S. S. (1992). A Ser/Ala polymorphism in red photopigment underlies variation in colour matching. *Nature*, *356*(6368), 431.

Yamaguchi, T., Motulsky, A. G., and Deeb, S. S. (1997). Visual pigment gene structure and expression in human retinae. *Human Molecular Genetics*, *6*(7), 981–990.

Yokoyama, S., and Radlwimmer, F. B. (1999). The molecular genetics of red and green color vision in mammals. *Genetics*, *153*(2), 919–932.

Zhao, Z., Hewett-Emmett, D., and Li, W. H. (1998). Frequent gene conversion between human red and green opsin genes. *Journal of Molecular Evolution*, *46*(4), 494–496.

Zhaoping, L., and Carroll, J. (2016). An analytical model of the influence of cone sensitivity and numerosity on the Rayleigh match. *Journal of the Optical Society of America A*, *33*(3), A228–A237.

Zhou, Y. H., Hewett-Emmett, D., Ward, J. P., and Li, W. H. (1997). Unexpected conservation of the X-linked color vision gene in nocturnal prosimians: Evidence from two bush babies. *Journal of Molecular Evolution*, *45*(6), 610–618.

Acknowledgments

Portions of these findings were presented at the Munsell Centennial Color Symposium: Bridging Science, Art, & Industry. June 10–15, 2018. Massachusetts College of Art and Design, Boston, MA, USA. This work was funded in part by the National Science Foundation (#SMA-1416907, PI Jameson); by the Discovery Eye Foundation (PIs Jameson and Kenney); and by a Francisco Ayala School of Biological Sciences/Medical School Faculty Pilot Research Award (PIs Jameson, Kenney, Briscoe). Opsin genotyping was performed at the Gavin Herbert Eye Institute, UC Irvine Medical School. Views and opinions expressed in this work are those of the authors and do not necessarily reflect the official policy or position of any agency of the University of California or the National Science Foundation. The authors appreciate the involvement of our research participants and acknowledge helpful suggestions provided by reviewers of the manuscript including M. A. Webster, G. V. Paramei, A. K. Romney, L. Narens, and D. Saari, and, in particular, J. T. Enns.

Cambridge Elements ≡

Perception

James T. Enns
The University of British Columbia

Editor James T. Enns is Professor at the University of British Columbia, where he researches the interaction of perception, attention, emotion, and social factors. He has previously been Editor of the *Journal of Experimental Psychology: Human Perception and Performance* and an Associate Editor at *Psychological Science, Consciousness and Cognition, Attention Perception & Psychophysics,* and *Visual Cognition.*

Editorial Board
Gregory Francis *Purdue University*
Kimberly A. Jameson *University of California, Irvine*
Tyler Lorig *Washington and Lee University*
Rob Gray *Arizona State University*
Salvador Soto-Faraco *Universitat Pompeu Fabra*

About the Series
The modern study of human perception includes event perception, bidirectional influences between perception and action, music, language, the integration of the senses, human action observation, and the important roles of emotion, motivation, and social factors. Each Element in the series combines authoritative literature reviews of foundational topics with forward-looking presentations of the recent developments on a given topic.

Cambridge Elements ☰

Perception

Lightning Source UK Ltd.
Milton Keynes UK
UKHW020902071022
409995UK00011B/138